TEACHER'S EDITION FOR

Partners with God

Irene Bolton

Rabbi William Cutter

Gila Gevirtz

Rabbi Jules Harlow

Frances B. Pearlman

Tamar Raff

Ruby G. Strauss

Jessica B. Weber

Rabbi David Wolpe

BEHRMAN HOUSE, INC.

INTRODUCTION

by Rabbi David Wolpe

We teach the holidays. We teach history. We teach about the Bible, about our land and language. But when it comes to teaching about God, we are often silent.

This silence is strange, since God is the source and authority behind the holidays we celebrate, the history and Bible we learn, and the rich mix of traditions and teaching we revere. God infuses all that we try to transmit to our students: we praise God before reading from the Torah, after eating a meal, as we usher in Shabbat; we build a *sukkah* and light candles and knead *hallah* in response to God's commands; God tells us to visit the sick, feed the hungry, and care for our world.

Yet an awareness of God is often missing from our religious school classes. We teach children how to behave and how to live Jewishly, but fail to teach them why. God is "why."

As Jews we have a rich legacy of teaching about the meaning of God. Thousands of years of experience have provided us with real answers to questions children pose: Does God have a body? Who were God's parents? Why does God allow bad things to happen? If God spoke to Abraham, why doesn't God speak to me?

We need to take full advantage of this legacy. *Our children* want to achieve an understanding of God and of holiness. *They want* to find a higher meaning for the things and creatures that inhabit our world. And we *should want* them to achieve this understanding, for many reasons:

Children need to learn how to be good. Judaism does not teach that people are either naturally good or naturally bad. Rather it teaches that people struggle between righteous and evil inclinations. From a young age children struggle with impulses of selfishness, cruelty, and anger. Goodness must be taught. That is why we are so pleased and proud when our children do act honorably— because goodness is difficult, and it deserves praise.

We need a source of moral rules. Our sense of morality—of right and wrong— underlies the rules we make for our own behavior, and for our children's. But why should we obey these rules? What makes us develop a moral sense that then restricts our personal freedom to do as we please? Is there a deeper reason than our own feelings or our need to please and conform to the standards of our neighbors?

Moral rules matter because they are greater than human invention. They are a Divine legacy. The sense of objective right and wrong is bequeathed to us by Judaism's insistence on the existence of one God passionately concerned about what we *do*. Human beings did not invent the laws, and human beings cannot repeal them. But it is our obligation to understand them, elaborate them, and live by them.

Jewish ritual is Jewish language. Ritual is a language we use to speak to God. Our ritual language is more than words; it involves gestures, nuances, and a delicate web of associations and memories. Like a spoken language, Jewish ritual is intricate and beautiful and capable of many shades of meaning. When we teach children how to light candles, we are teaching them to say something to God that words alone cannot express.

Ritual is also a language in which we speak to each other as well as to the generations of Jews who preceded us. The rabbis of the Talmud teach that *mitzvot* were given to "refine human beings" (*Bereshit Rabbah 44:1*). If we can teach our students to talk to God and to each other in this way, we will have given them a lifelong means to develop their souls.

We build self-esteem through our knowledge of God. We all want our children to value themselves. Yet it is difficult to nurture a child's self-worth given that life is so complex and uncertain. Basing self-esteem on a child's talents or accomplishments—implicitly placing a value on a child by comparing him or her to others—invites conceit and self-pity, for there will always be people of lesser and greater talents. We do not want children's self-esteem to be based solely on what another person thinks or does, be that person a peer, a coach, a teacher, or a parent.

While the changing nature of human perspectives and experiences cannot anchor self-esteem, the knowledge that we are all created in God's image, *b'tzelem Elohim*, can. Being created in the image of God is permanent—in good times and bad, when one feels loved or when one feels lost. What could be more bracing than to know that you were created in the image of God, the Holy One, the Sovereign of the Universe? Being created in God's image makes a person invaluable. And as teachers, we can see God's image in the faces of our students—spiritual lives entrusted to us.

We feel holiness through our knowledge of God. By teaching our students about God, we give them the opportunity to feel a sense of the sacred. Holiness is about things that are greater than us but that are still a part of us. Connecting to God is how we Jews bring a sense of holiness into our lives and into this world.

We build continuity and community through our knowledge of God. Why have Jews survived for so long? How are we connected to other Jews across time and across the world? We have survived because of the powerful call Jews have felt to honor God and to carry out Judaism's mission: *L'taken olam b'malchut Shaddai*—to repair the world under the Sovereignty of God.

We are connected to each other, and to our past, by the same powerful call. It is what connects us to the newly freed slaves of the Bible, to the Talmudic Jews of Babylonia, to the Jewish grape growers in medieval France, and to the Eastern European *shtetl* forebears of the nineteenth century. They were all imbued with this passion to honor God and to improve God's world.

Throughout their lives, our children will be questioned and challenged in their beliefs as Jews. Let us now teach them that they are heirs to a people that first introduced knowledge of God to humanity. Let us now teach them that they are, indeed, partners with God.

How To Use This Guide

The following descriptions will help you make best use of the materials presented in this guide:

Teaching Goals
The overall teaching objectives for each chapter to help the teacher plan the lessons

How to Get Started
Practical suggestions for introducing each chapter in the text (Set Induction)

Things to Talk About
Key discussion points to emphasize primary material in the text

Take a Closer Look
Opportunities to expand and enhance students' understanding of important concepts

How to Teach the Story
Background information for the teacher and ways to enrich the reading of the story

Activity Suggestion
A wide variety of activities to use in the classroom and at home

Use the Photograph
Techniques for using the photographs to promote students' critical thinking

A Note to the Teacher
Interesting facts, special teaching opportunities, and textual cross-references

Teach the Hebrew Lesson
Suggestions for teaching the Hebrew vocabulary in the text

From the Rabbi's Desk
Rabbi David Wolpe's ongoing commentary

Partners withGod

Gila Gevirtz

EDITORIAL COMMITTEE

Chair: Rabbi Jules Harlow

Rabbi Morrison D. Bial
Rabbi Eugene B. Borowitz
Rabbi Nina Beth Cardin
Rabbi William Cutter

Dr. Tikva Frymer-Kensky
Rabbi Arthur Green
Dr. Barry Holtz
Rabbi David Wolpe

BEHRMAN HOUSE, INC.

Our modern world does not seem to leave much room for God. We function day to day in the realm of concrete facts. Which blessing do we say when eating raisins? What exactly did happen as we left Egypt? We don't speak much about the Divine. As a third grader said, "It's hard to know God because God is something you can't know. It's not like knowing your math facts."

Each of us experiences God in a unique manner. Some feel God's presence each and every moment, some have had one or two special moments in a lifetime, and some are still waiting for that moment to come. Since this is true of children as well as adults, the presentation of the material in this book is at once challenging and exciting for you, the teacher. Each student and each teacher will approach this subject with his or her own outlook, own sense of the Divine.

In choosing *Partners with God*, you have chosen to help your students "make room" for God in their lives. And as they learn to reach higher and higher toward God, may they come to realize that they have embarked on the lifelong process that we call Judaism.

DEDICATION

In memory of my parents,
Gertrude and Hyman Gevirtz, ז״ל
Two very different people, they both contributed
greatly to my love of God, Torah, and Israel, and
to my understanding of life as creative process.
G.G.

ACKNOWLEDGMENTS

Ruby Strauss is a dynamic and artful editor whose vision, insight,
integrity, and good humor are woven into each page of this book.
She is a blessing and I feel blessed.

Special thanks to the many students, educators, scholars, parents,
and rabbis who generously contributed to the development of
Partners with God.

PROJECT EDITOR: RUBY G. STRAUSS

BOOK DESIGN: ROBERT J. O'DELL

ARTISTS: BRYNA WALDMAN, JONI LEVY LIBERMAN, LARRY NOLTE

PHOTO CREDITS

Photo Researcher: Lynn Goldberg Biderman

COVER: Pete Saloutos/The Stock Market. FPG INTERNATIONAL 6 Ron Chapple. 14 Arthur Tilley. 34 Jacob Taposchaner. 20 Arthur Tilley. 32 Walter Chorazuewicz. 135 Jade Albert. THE STOCK MARKET 4 Ken Moreck. 10 Vince Streano. 12 Charles Krebs. 53 Peter Augelo Simon. 57 Ed Bock. 64 Arni Skolley. 73 Mug Shots. 70 Mug Shots. 77 David Woods. 79 Dimaggio/Kalish. 82 Mug Shots. 94 Tom and Dewnni McCarthy. 98 Bill Binzen. 122 Jose L. Pelaez. 118 George Disario. 129 Paul Barton. 122 Paul Barton. FRANCENE KEERY 15, 73, 149. SUPERSTOCK 29 T. Rosenthal. 36 Superstock. 38 T. Rosenthal. 39 T. Jones. 42 F.B. Productions. 46 T. Rosenthal. 48 F.B. Productions. 72 L. Prince. 76 A. Bosco. 88 S. Wickers. 101 Superstock. 102 R Heymans. 110 T. Cnowse. PHOTO RESEARCHERS 24 Phillip Hayson. 66 Tony Wayd. 60 Andy Levin. 129 George Holton. BIBLICAL ARCHAEOLOGY SOCIETY 56. ILENE PERLMAN 58. HEBREW UNION COLLEGE SKIRBALL MUSEUM. 67. Gat LAS MUSEUM OF ART, MUNGER FUND 94 Camille Pissarro "Apple Picking at Eragny-sur-Epte". COMSTOCK 100. THE IMAGE BANK 106 Gary Kufner. ZEPHYR PICTURES 120 P. Skinner

© COPYRIGHT 1995 BY GILA GEVIRTZ
PUBLISHED BY BEHRMAN HOUSE, INC.
235 Watchung Avenue, West Orange, New Jersey 07052
ISBN 0-87441-580-2 (Paperback)
ISBN 0-87441-594-2 (Hardcover)
MANUFACTURED IN THE UNITED STATES OF AMERICA

CONTENTS

3

A Note to the teacher

Did you ever consider the Table of Contents as a teaching tool? Think about using this page to introduce your students to what they will be learning in *Partners with God* and to help them see how the book is organized.

For example, you might ask how the book is divided, the names of the two parts, on which page Chapter 11 begins, etc. Then you might consider asking the students to pick the chapter title that looks most interesting to them and give them a few moments to look through that chapter. This is a nice way to have students discover the varied elements in each chapter (photographs, stories, art, activities, sidebars, etc.).

Create a "Partners with God" Observation Window

Choose a window (in your classroom, in the sanctuary, or somewhere else in the building) to be the window through which the class will periodically observe and record God's presence in the world. Be sure to select a window with a nice view—overlooking a grassy area (not the parking lot); with a view of nature (not the trash containers). Make a sign to hang over the window: "Discovering God's World" or "Looking at God's World." Throughout the year, spend some special moments looking through the window to observe and record the changes from season to season, e.g., colorful leaves in the fall, snow-covered ground in winter, birds and budding trees and flowers in spring, etc. Record the observations and post them next to the window.

Encourage your students to designate a similar observation window at home.

"One should always pray in a room that has windows."

Talmud: Brachot 34b

PART ONE

Discovering God's World

This book was written just for you. It was written because you have important questions you want answered, such as "Is it possible to see God?" "Does God care about me?" and "How can I be 'God's partner'?"

These questions are so important they have been asked over and over again for thousands of years. Our ancestors Abraham and Sarah, who lived in the time of the Bible, were the first to ask these questions. The Children of Israel asked the same questions as they followed Moses out of Egypt and through the wilderness. And generations

4

later, the Jews who hid while knights on horseback rode through their towns asked these questions too.

The same important questions were asked by the early Jewish settlers in America who helped George Washington and Abraham Lincoln fight for freedom and equality. And they were asked again by your great great grandparents who taught their children and their children's children to continue questioning.

Every generation of the Jewish people has continued to ask questions about God. Each generation has searched for answers in the wisdom of our tradition. And each generation has added its own understanding of God to the tradition.

Now it is your turn. Now *you* will explore the Jewish tradition and add *your* wisdom to our understanding of God. You will share the experience with your teacher, your classmates, and your family. And you will have special moments that are yours alone.

As you read *Partners with God*, you will discover much about the goodness and beauty of God's world and what it means to live as a Jew. You will read many stories that teach you about God's love and how the Jewish people were born. As you think about what you read and as you share with others, you will find answers to many of your questions.

Come, let us go now and explore God's world together. Let us join the generations of our people and discover what we can about God.

5

Create a Question Box

Put a cardboard box in the class-room with a slit cut in the top. Label the box: "Questions about God." Explain to the students that they may write questions they have about God on pieces of paper and put them in the box at any time during the year. (Be sure to check the box at the end of each class session and respond to the students' questions at the next meeting when appropriate.)

Teaching Goals

After studying this chapter, the student will understand:

1. We cannot know what God looks like, but we can see the things that God creates.

2. God's creations are like footprints, signs of God's presence.

3. The fact that we cannot see something does not mean it is not there.

Although you cannot see the wind, you know it's there when it carries your kite high up in the sky.

Can you think of something else you cannot see, but you know is there?

6

How We Know God

Have you ever wondered what God looks like? Whether God gets wet when it rains or warm when the sun shines? Do you think God has ears to hear your prayers or a mouth to answer them?

Maybe you've heard God called the Creator and you pictured an artist wearing a smock with bright red splotches of paint on it. Or perhaps you read a prayer in which God is called our Father and you imagined a loving parent with laughing eyes and a tender smile.

7

From the Rabbi's Desk

Light cannot be seen. What we see is not light, but light bouncing off other things—walls, clothes, faces, even particles in the air. The same is true of God. We cannot see God. God becomes real through the beauty of the world, through the actions of people.

Just as with light, although we cannot see God, we can know God and bring God into this world. I cannot show you goodness, but I can show you an act of goodness. I cannot show you God, but an act of godliness makes God somehow tangible.

—DJW

Before class begins, prepare one index card for each student in your class. Write one of the following questions on each card:

When do you think about God?

What do you believe about God?

What do you wonder about God?

Hand one card to each student as she or he enters the classroom and ask your students to write a one-sentence answer. (Several students will have the same question. This will help to demonstrate that there can be more than one "correct" answer.)

Collect and shuffle the cards. Read a few student responses aloud and talk about them.

Be sure to explain that you too have questions about God. Being Jewish means that we are encouraged to ask a lot of questions. Sometimes we find answers in our tradition, and sometimes we find that we are led to even more questions. As we grow up, we learn how important it is to ask more questions and to keep looking for answers. This process brings us closer to God.

Conclude the exercise by explaining that this book will answer some of their questions about God and will help them develop a better understanding of their relationship with God. Say: "This first chapter will help us find the answer to a very difficult question: How do we know God?"

We can smell the sweet fragrance of a flower, but what does the smell of a flower look like?

Can your students name other things that are real but don't have shapes or forms that we can see (e.g., emotions such as happiness and sadness)?

We may know that people feel happy when they smile, but can we see the "feeling"?

Activity Suggestion

Ask students to draw a picture of "love" or to find a picture in a magazine or among their personal photos that shows that love is real.

Display students' pictures on the bulletin board under the heading: "God's Love is Real."

The wind is real but it doesn't have a shape. Love is real but it doesn't have a form or a body. What kind of picture would you draw to show that love is real?

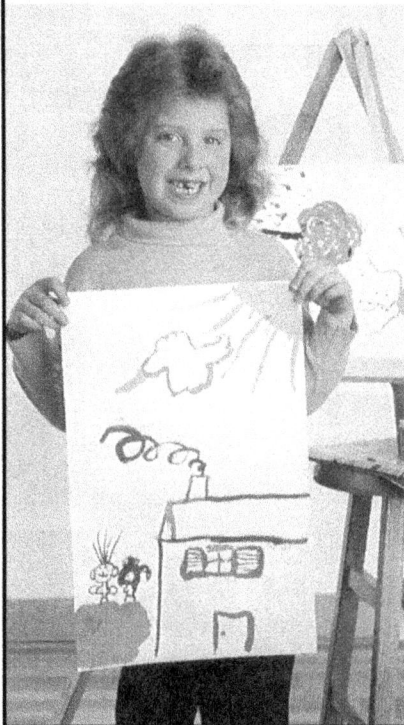

Or maybe you chanted a blessing, or *brachah*, in which God is called King, and you thought it meant that God is a powerful ruler with gray hair and long flowing robes.

The truth is that God is not a person and does not look like one. God does not look like a mother or a father, a king or a queen. God doesn't have a body or a face—no mouth, eyes, ears, or nose. God is not short or tall, thin or fat, young or old.

"Then what does God look like?" you ask.

The answer is, we don't know. We cannot see God. We can only see what God creates.

❖   ❖   ❖

This girl worked hard on her painting and she is proud of it. Have you ever created a picture or a poem of which you were proud? Did you share it with others?

God created the oceans we swim in, the trees that provide us with shade and sweet fruit, and the flowers that fill our gardens. How does it feel to share these and God's many other creations?

8

Take a Closer Look

After reading this page, consider the descriptions of God in the text (Creator, Father, Ruler), then ask students to add others (Judge, Helper, Teacher, etc.). List them all on the chalkboard.

Ask:

Why do you think we give God names such as Creator, Father, Ruler?

Do these words help us to make a picture in our minds about God?

Do you think it helps some people to have a picture of God in their minds?

Does it help them to pray?

Are these pictures true? Can they mislead us? How?

An Interesting Question

Rabbi Akiba was one of the wisest teachers of the Jewish people. One day a man who did not believe in God came to him and said, "I have heard that you believe God created the wonders of the world. Tell me, what proof do you have that it is so?"

"An interesting question," said Akiba. "But before I answer you, I must know one thing. You're wearing a most splendid outfit. Can you tell me who made the material?"

"A weaver, of course," replied the man, surprised by the question.

"Really!" said Akiba. "What is your proof?"

The man became confused. "I don't know what you mean, rabbi. What kind of proof do you want? Isn't it clear that all cloth is made by a weaver?"

"Certainly," said Akiba. "And isn't it just as clear that all the wonders of the world were made by God?"

9

How to Teach the Story

An Interesting Question

Read the opening paragraph of the story aloud to the class. Ask your students what proof they would give to the man who didn't believe in God. Then read the complete story together.

Ask:

Do you think that Rabbi Akiba's answer is convincing proof? Why or why not?

Act It Out

This story will work well as a student "playlet" with three characters: Akiba, the man, a narrator.

Create a New Story

Explain to your students: This story is about proving that God exists. This has always been an important question to people. Ask: Why do you think that is so? Encourage the class to create a story similar to Rabbi Akiba's. Begin with: "A man came up to me and said, "'I hear that you believe in God. What proof do you have?'"

A Note to the Teacher

As a young man, Akiba was a shepherd. Although he yearned to study Torah, he could not because he didn't know how to read or write. When his son started school, Akiba decided to join him and together they learned the *alef bet*.

The more Akiba learned, the more he wanted to know. And so he continued to study, year after year, until he became a great rabbi and one of the wisest teachers of the Jewish people.

(Avot d'Rabbi Natan Ch. 6)

Take a Closer Look

A philosopher, Bahya ibn Pakuda, offered a similar proof which you might like to share with your students.

Bahya said, "If, by accident, ink spilled out onto a blank sheet of paper, the result would never be legible writing. Who would believe someone who showed us a page of beautifully written script and said it resulted from an ink spill? How, then, can anyone claim that the world, which is so much more intricate in its design than a page of writing, came about without the purpose and power of a creator?"

How is Akiba's proof similar to this one?

Things to Talk About

Ask students to share times when they could have thanked God for something good in their lives.

Use the Photograph

Look at the picture of the giraffes. The giraffe is an example of one of God's creations. Ask the class to name others that are not listed in the text.

Explain that each of God's creations is unique and specially suited for life on earth. Ask how the giraffe is unique and specially suited for life on earth.

The man could think of no reply. Humbly, he thanked the rabbi and bid him goodbye.

Rabbi Akiba turned to his students—who had overheard the conversation—and explained, "It is well to remember that everything has a creator. When you see cloth you know that a weaver wove it. When you see a house, you know a builder built it. And when you see a door, you know that a carpenter made it.

"In the same way," Akiba went on, "when you see the natural wonders of the world you know they too have a creator—God."

❖　　❖　　❖

God's wonders are all around us. Draw one creation that is a favorite of yours. Write one reason why you love it so much.

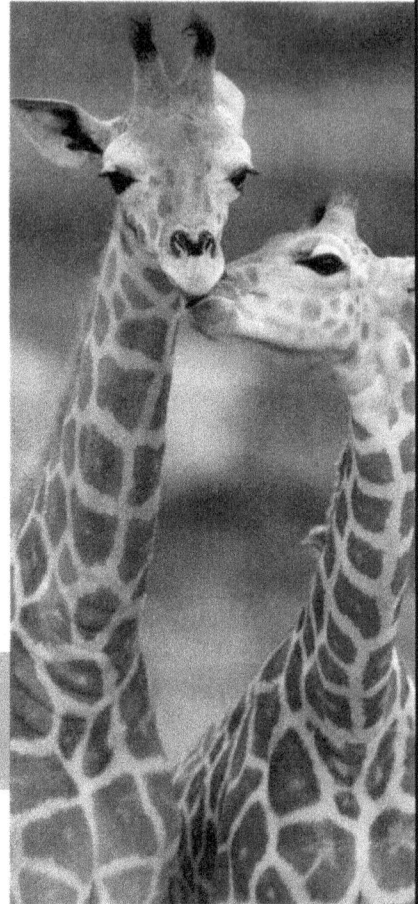

10

Activity Suggestion

Ask students to find three things at home that were made by people and to write a description of what they are and who made them.

Then suggest that they take a walk through their neighborhoods to find three things that were created by God, to list them, and to write a description of what the world might be like if God had not made those creations (e.g., if there were no rain, we would run out of water to drink and plants could not grow).

God's Footprints

The list of God's creations is very long. Birds that fly and insects that crawl. Cherries that bob in tall leafy trees and carrots that push through the dark soil below. Turtles that tuck their small heads in shells and giraffes that S-T-R-E-T-C-H their long spotted necks.

Flowers and sunshine, rivers and rain forests, seashells and summertime—God created all these wonders of nature and much, much more.

Like footprints that are the telltale signs of a person we do not see, each of these creations reminds us that God is present in the world.

HEBREW LESSON

Baruch Atah — בָּרוּךְ אַתָּה
"Blessed are You"

At home or in the synagogue we recite blessings to thank God for the goodness in our lives. Reciting a blessing, a *brachah*, is one way we can talk to God. And just as we begin a letter to a friend by writing "Dear _____," or begin a telephone conversation by saying "Hello," so we begin a *brachah* by saying "Blessed are You."

11

Take a Closer Look

Ask the students who we are referring to when we say *Baruch atah*. (Be sure the class understands that we are *thanking* God rather than blessing God.)

Give each child a *siddur* and see how many times they can find the words *Baruch atah*.

Teach the Hebrew Lesson

This is the first of seven Hebrew lessons in *Partners with God*. These lessons have been included to give the students a basic Jewish vocabulary for talking about God. Additionally, other Hebrew terms in transliteration are in the text's narrative. The Hebrew words have been selected on the basis of their fundamental importance to understanding our partnership with God.

Here are a few suggestions for teaching the Hebrew vocabulary:

1. Create a bulletin board or other display for the Hebrew vocabulary that is introduced in the book. Display each word as it is introduced so that the class has a permanent visual of the words as they accumulate.

2. Use the vocabulary words actively and continually in classroom discussion. Ask your students to try doing so also. For example, instead of saying prayer, say *tefillah*. Use the word *emunah* instead of faith, *neshamah* instead of soul, etc.

3. After four or five words have been accumulated, play games with the vocabulary. Here are two suggestions:

Concentration: Make two identical sets of flashcards containing the vocabulary words. Place them face down on a table, in random order. Each student picks two, looking for a pair. If they find a pair, they read and translate the word correctly. Then they may keep the pair. The one with the most pairs at the end of the game is the winner.

Act Out: One student comes forward and acts out the word of his or her choice. The others guess what it might be. The first one to get the correct answer acts out the next word.

Even when the jet plane flies higher and we can no longer see it, we can know it is there by the trail it leaves behind. In the same way, the natural wonders of our world form a trail that reminds us of God's presence.

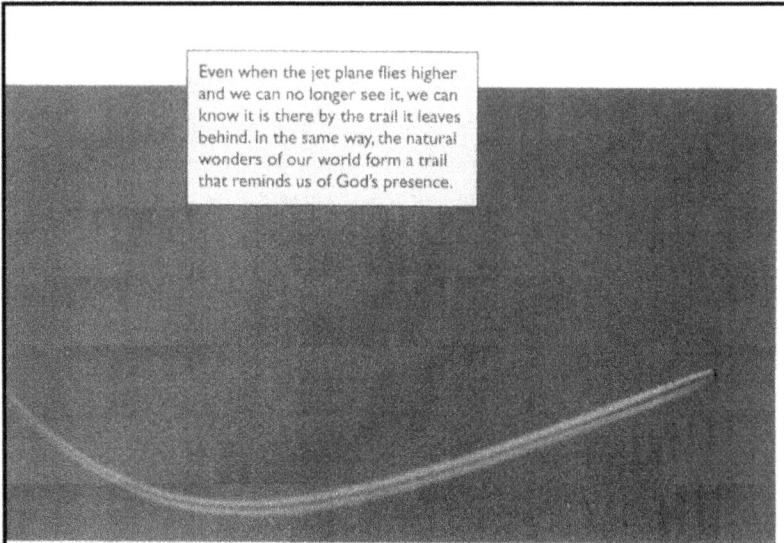

SEEING IS BELIEVING

Not everything that is real can be seen. You know the wind is real, but you cannot see it. Feelings are real but they cannot be seen. There are signs that help us know that the wind is blowing and that people are feeling a certain way. For example, when you see a person smile, you know that person feels happy.

Complete these sentences:

When I see _____, I know it is windy outside.

When I see _____, I know someone feels sad.

When I see _____, I know it rained during the night.

When I see _____, I know there's a fire burning nearby.

When I see _____, I know it's time to celebrate Ḥanukkah.

When I see _____, I know it's someone's birthday.

When I see _____, I know God is present.

12

SIMPLY INDESCRIBABLE!

Are there people, places, and things you find difficult to describe? Are there times when it helps to compare them to something else?

Maybe you know someone who runs around "like a chicken without its head," or perhaps you've seen a house so large and beautiful that it looks "like a palace."

Describe the following person, place, and thing by comparing each to someone or something else. For example, you might say, "My school is as busy as a beehive," "When I swim, I feel like a fish," and "My bed feels as warm as toast."

1. My school is as

_____

as _____ .

2. When I _____ ,

I feel like _____ .

3. My bed feels as _____

as _____ .

Because God cannot be seen, it is difficult to describe God. Sometimes it helps to compare God to people, places, and things we can see. That is why when we want to describe how powerful God is, we may call God a "Ruler." When we want to describe how caring God is, we may call God a "Shepherd" and call people "God's flock."

How would you describe God? What would you compare God to?

1. God is as

_____

as _____ .

2. God is

_____

like _____ .

13

Things to Talk About

Ask the students to share the answers they wrote on the bottom of page 13. Discuss why different people describe God in different ways.

Teaching Goals

After studying this chapter, the student will understand:

1. God is always with us.
2. If we learn to "pay attention," we can become more aware of God's presence in our lives. We must learn "to let God in."
3. God is found in nature, in the miracle of growth, and in relationships between people.
4. We cannot hide from God.

April showers are gentle and refreshing. The cool water feels good against our skin. Each drop is like a miracle—adding water to our oceans, satisfying our thirst, and helping our gardens grow. Because we use water every day, we sometimes take it for granted. But water is a precious gift, like the air we breathe. What other gifts are part of your daily life?

14

CHAPTER 2

Where We Find God

Do snowy days sometimes make you shiver on the outside but smile on the inside? Does the sound of thunder crashing through the sky fill your heart with awe and wonder? Can the sight of lightning bugs glowing in the dark turn an ordinary evening into one that seems quite *extraordinary*?

These are but a few of nature's delights that can add joy and excitement to our everyday lives. Of course, if we're not paying attention we won't notice them. We might even think that nothing good or interesting ever happens.

15

How to Get Started

Before beginning the chapter, it might be nice to visit the synagogue sanctuary, if possible. Sit quiety and carefully look around, or have students close their eyes and listen to the silence in the sanctuary. Ask the students if they feel God in this place.

Ask students to complete this sentence: God is present when . . .

or

I think about God when . . .

or

Something I wonder about God is . . . .

From the Rabbi's Desk

There are many places to find God in the world. We can find God in the origins of things—at births and beginnings. We can find God in the beauty of the world. We can find God in sacred moments, when we gather together to celebrate or even to grieve. And we can find God in one another—we are created in the image of God, and so each person is a reflection of the Divine.

—DJW

Take a Closer Look

When you play with a toy or game that belongs to someone else, how can you take care of it in a way that shows respect for the other person?

Activity Suggestion

Darken the classroom, sit on the floor close together, and describe the following sounds to the students: children laughing, birds singing, a babbling brook, a *shofar* blast, etc. (If you can obtain recorded sounds, so much the better.)

Discuss how each of these sounds can remind us to be aware of God's presence.

Things to Talk About

Ask your students if they have ever sat in a classroom during a lesson and not paid attention to the teacher. Or perhaps their parents asked them to clean their room or set the dinner table and they weren't listening. Have them give other examples of times they paid close attention and times they didn't pay any attention at all. Discuss what it means to pay attention. How is this done? Can it be done in different ways? When are you most or least successful?

It's the same way with us and God. When we pay attention, we become aware that God is always present. When we don't pay attention, it seems as if God is never around.

You don't need to go far to see the work of God. God has no special address or hideaway. God can be found everywhere, any time—morning, noon, and night.

Feeling God's Presence

When you pay attention, you will notice that many moments are filled with God's presence. You can feel it in the quiet of a silent prayer or in the twinkle of a star. You can know God is present as the seasons dress the earth in a wardrobe of autumn leaves, winter snow, spring blossoms, and summer harvest. And you can be aware of God's work as you watch yourself become taller, smarter, and more grown up.

You can also feel God's presence when people treat each other with kindness and respect. On a bus, when someone gives an older person a seat, God is present. In school, when you smile and welcome a new student, God is present. And at home, when you help your mom or dad clean up or when you thank others for *their* help, God is present.

> Did something wonderful happen today that you didn't pay attention to? Were you too busy or too much in a hurry to notice? What can you do next time to help you pay attention?

Sometimes you may not be in the mood to be caring or loving. You may feel a bit cranky or lazy, or angry with a friend. But a quiet, gentle voice deep inside you may tell you to clean up your room without being asked, or to try a little harder at school, or to call the friend with whom you are angry and say, "I miss you." When that happens, God is present. You can be sure of it because you feel

16

Activity Suggestion

Ask students to make a list of times they notice God's presence. For example, they may notice God's presence when they see a beautiful flower or sunset, or when someone smiles at them. Tell them to write what happened, when it happened, and where, and to bring the list to the next class session.

good inside. God's presence is that quiet, gentle voice that helps you do good and feel good.

When you want a reminder of God's presence, just look out your window or walk outside and enjoy God's creations. God can be found everywhere.

> Some people feel very close to God in the synagogue.
> Some feel close to God when they stand outside on a starry night.
> Where do you feel closest to God?

17

Use the Photograph

A synagogue sanctuary is a prayer space designed with God in mind. The space, sound, furniture, and holy objects chosen help us concentrate on God's presence. Ask the students to describe some of the things that make your synagogue sanctuary feel holy. Why has the community created this special place to pray? How do these things help us to pay attention to God's presence?

Activity Suggestion

Disposable cameras are readily available and reasonably priced. Depending on your budget, bring one or several to class. The students can share them, each taking a few pictures on the roll of film that comes in the camera.

Take a group walk. As you go, photograph "things" that help us feel God's presence in the world. Or, allow each student to take a camera home to take two or three pictures before passing the camera along to a classmate.

Display the developed photographs on the bulletin board. If cameras aren't available, the display can be made of pictures cut from magazines, or use children's drawings.

Things to Talk About

When do we feel God's presence? Point out to your students that Jewish people bring God into their lives by performing *mitzvot* or commandments. Some of these are listed in the text, such as giving an older person a seat or helping parents with chores. Ask your students to list other *mitzvot* that might help us to feel God's presence. Examples might be lighting Shabbat candles and praying. Why do these things make us aware of God's presence? (When we act the way God wants us to act, God becomes a part of our lives.)

❓ Things to Talk About

The students are learning that the world can tell us a great deal about God.

Ask students what their rooms "say" about them. Encourage them to talk about particular items or objects that can help us know more about them.

Continue the discussion with this question: What creations "speak" to you about God? What do they "say"?

A Note to the Teacher

You may want to explain to your students that the Tree of Knowledge is "the Tree of Knowledge of Good and Bad" (*Genesis 2:17*).

A rabbi once asked a group of learned visitors, "Where is God?" Surprised by his question, the guests immediately answered, "God is everywhere, of course." The rabbi shook his head and said, "No, my friends. God is wherever we let God in."

> The Torah tells the story of how Adam and Eve ate the fruit of the Tree of Knowledge, the tree God had commanded them not to touch. Ashamed, they tried to hide from God.
> There are times when each of us may be tempted to do something we know we should not do. Feeling guilty or ashamed, or hoping to avoid our responsibilities, we may try to hide from God.
> Do you think we can succeed? Why or why not?

We must be willing to pay attention to the world and to the people around us. And we must be willing to see God's loving kindness and add to that kindness by the way we treat others. We must be willing to listen to that quiet, gentle voice inside us and to let God in everywhere.

❖   ❖   ❖

Jonah Learns a Lesson

The Bible teaches us about Jonah, a prophet of Israel who thought he could run away from God, and from his responsibilities, by sailing to a far-off land.

As Jonah set sail, God sent a strong wind and a mighty storm that threatened to swallow the ship and all its passengers. Frightened, the sailors prayed to their gods. But their prayers did not help— the storm raged on as before.

Finally the sailors cried out in despair, "Let us cast lots that we may know who brought this trouble on us." So they cast lots— and the lot fell on Jonah.

Turning to Jonah, the sailors asked, "What must we do to calm the sea?"

And Jonah replied, "Take me up and throw me overboard. Only then will you be safe."

18

How to Teach the Story

Jonah Learns a Lesson

Jonah was a prophet. God decided to send Jonah to the city of Nineveh to tell the people who lived in the city that they would be destroyed unless they renounced their evil ways. Instead, Jonah boarded a ship at Jaffa bound for Tarshish, which is in the opposite direction from Nineveh.

After the story has been read, ask your students if they remember what happened to Jonah after he was thrown into the sea.

Can they tell the rest of the story?

Point out to the class that Jonah could not hide from the responsibilities that God assigned to him. Explain that sometimes God gives us important jobs to do. Ask what we should do when this happens to us. (Give specific examples. For example, suppose a child gets hurt on the playground. Do you ignore him and continue playing, or do you go for help?)

Being aware of God's presence gives us confidence. Ask the students about some of the new challenges they will face in the future. Can God help them to have the strength and confidence to succeed at them?

Now the sailors were kind people, and at first they refused to throw Jonah overboard. But the storm raged on and on, so at last they threw him into the sea. And as they did, the sea became calm once more.

In the end, God saved Jonah and Jonah learned that we cannot hide from God. God is everywhere—on land and at sea.

It is wonderful to learn how to do new things. And the older you become, the more things you will be able to do. Being aware of God's caring presence can fill you with the confidence you need to learn new skills and enjoy new experiences.

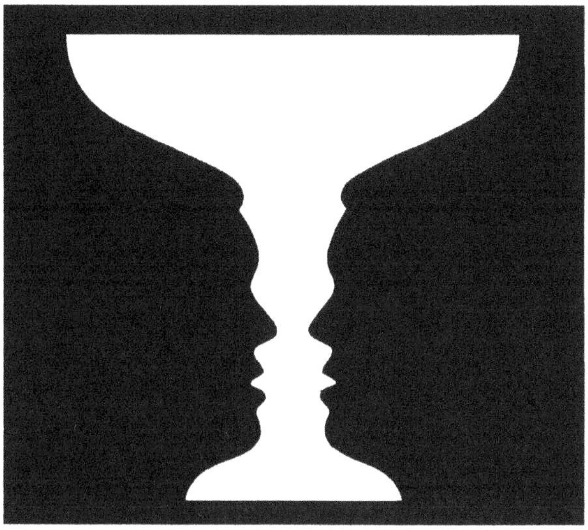

ATTENTION!

Look at the picture above. What do you see?
Do you see a wine cup or two faces looking at each other?
Can you see both?
It all depends on whether you look at the white shape
or at the black shapes.

In the same way, we can become more aware of
God's presence when we pay close attention to the
world around us.

21

Things to Talk About

Some people see the wine cup in the picture and some don't. Some people feel God's presence and some have not yet learned how to perceive it. Ask the children to think of times and places where different people see the same event and yet perceive it differently. (Example: During a prayer service, some people speak sincerely to God and some people just read words. During a football game, some people feel the excitement of every play and some people just see a ball being thrown around.)

BE AWARE!

Name three things you were not able to do last year that you can do now.

I can_____
_____

I can_____
_____

I can_____
_____

Name two things you look forward to doing when you are older.

I can't wait to _____
_____

    when I am_____ years-old.

I can't wait to _____
_____

    when I am_____ years-old.

22

AN IMPORTANT LESSON

Jonah learned an important lesson.
What is the most important lesson
you have learned about God in the
first two chapters of this book?
Write it on the lines.

THINK ABOUT IT

Think of one moment in your life when you felt that
God was present. What were you doing?

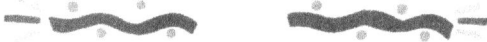

23

After studying this chapter, the student will understand:

1. The first story in the Torah tells us about the creation of the world.
2. We are partners with God.
3. All the people of the earth are related.

Each of us is a partner with God in caring for the world.
You can plant a tree and help it grow.
What else can you do to help take care of the world?

24

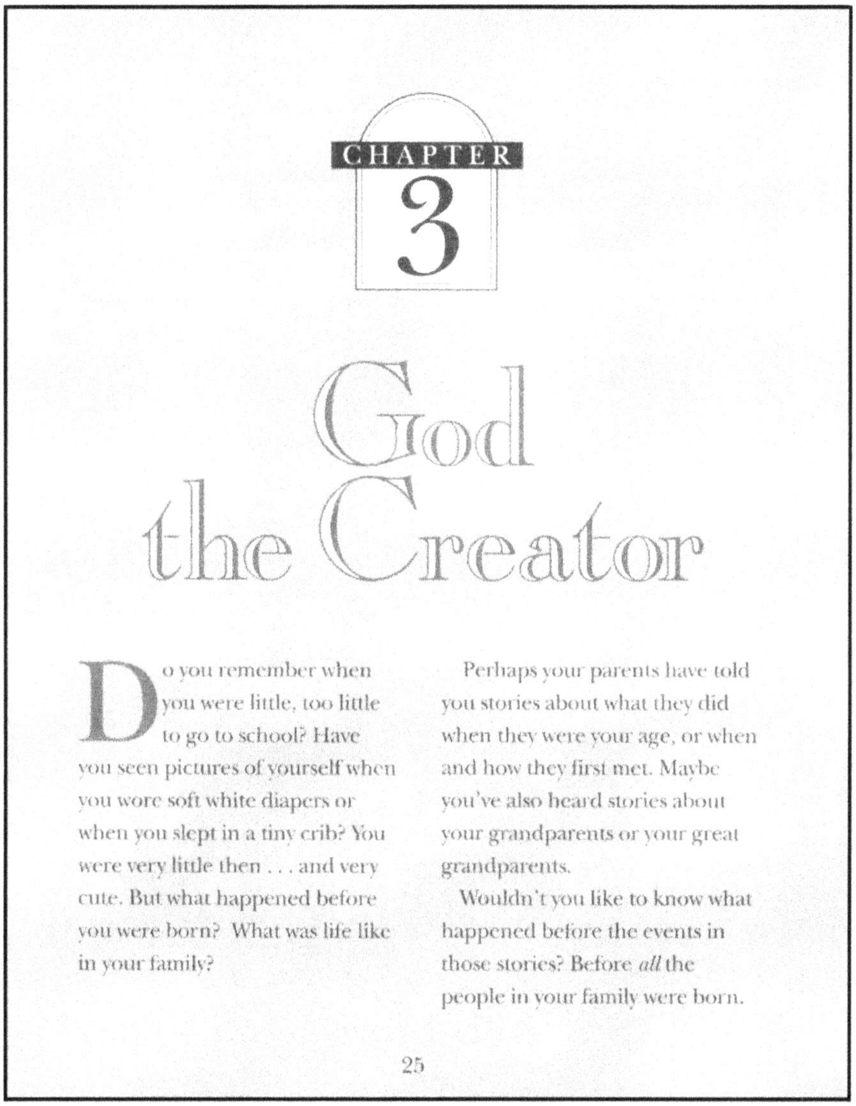

CHAPTER 3

God the Creator

Do you remember when you were little, too little to go to school? Have you seen pictures of yourself when you wore soft white diapers or when you slept in a tiny crib? You were very little then . . . and very cute. But what happened before you were born? What was life like in your family?

Perhaps your parents have told you stories about what they did when they were your age, or when and how they first met. Maybe you've also heard stories about your grandparents or your great grandparents.

Wouldn't you like to know what happened before the events in those stories? Before *all* the people in your family were born.

25

How to Get Started

Suggest that children bring in photographs of themselves as babies or toddlers and of other family members. Have them show the pictures to the class and tell some favorite family stories. Even if they don't bring pictures to class, students should be encouraged to share stories about their families.

From the Rabbi's Desk

We not only want to ask our students questions, we want to encourage them to ask questions as well. When children ask questions, doing so helps train them to look for God in their lives.

The Nobel Prize-winning physicist I.I. Rabi once told an interviewer that his most important intellectual influence was his mother. Each day when Rabi came home from school, his mother would say to him, "Isaac, did you ask any good questions today?" From that, said Rabi, he learned that the key to life was curiosity and wonder about the world.

—DJW

The Story of Creation

Ask your students to imagine a time before Creation when there was nothing. Is it difficult to do this? Why? God can create things out of nothing, unlike people, who can create one thing only from another. What are some examples of human creations as opposed to God's creations?

Before *all* the people in *all* the families in *the whole world* were born.

Fortunately, like the members of your family—from one generation to the next—Jewish teachers, or sages, have passed on those stories. Here's one story that may already have been passed on to you. It is written in the Torah.

Science teaches us how the world was created. It teaches us that huge dinosaurs once roamed the earth long before there were people and that it took billions of years to create the world and all its wonders.

The Torah teaches us why the world was created. It teaches us that God's goodness can be seen in the wonders of Creation and that human beings were made to care for God's world and for one another.

The Story of Creation

Long, long ago, before the mountains were born, there were no oceans to be sailed or brightly colored rainbows to be seen.

There were no stars to glitter and sparkle in the sky. There was no sun to spread its golden light and warmth over the earth. There was nothing to be seen or heard anywhere. God's goodness and love filled the universe, but there were no creatures—neither animals nor people—to enjoy that love and goodness.

26

Take a Closer Look

Ask students to name some natural wonders of the world created by God. List them, and then ask students if they would like to live in the world without these creations.

Then, in the beginning, the world was born as God created heaven and earth. On the first day God created the light, called Day, and the darkness, called Night. On the second day, the Sky was created. On the third day God created the Land, Seas, and Plants, and on the fourth day the Sun, the Moon and Stars. On the fifth day

Birds and Fish were created. And on the sixth day God created Cattle, Insects, and Wild Beasts.

God was pleased with all these creations. Where once there had been silence, now there were the gentle splash of summer rain and the mighty roar of ocean waves. Color burst forth from every form of life and the honeyed scent of

27

? Things to Talk About

Ask the students if they believe the world came into being just the way the Torah describes. Are they familiar with the widely accepted "Big Bang" theory, which holds that the universe began with a single huge explosion billions of years ago? Have they learned about the theory of evolution? Are these scientific theories at complete odds with the Torah account?

Instead of trying to translate advanced science back into the language of the Bible, help your students see that the Torah is not concerned with *how* the world was created, but rather with the moral order of the world. The significance of the Creation story is not in the details (if the Bible were written today and scientists contributed to the story of creation, the details would of course be different). The significance of the story lies in the understanding of our place in Creation and our responsibility to the world and to one another.

▨ Activity Suggestion

Make a "Creation" poster or bulletin board. Divide the area into categories of Day 1, Day 2, etc., and ask students to bring in pictures (cut from magazines or hand drawn) of creations that God made on each of the six days. Paste the creations on the appropriate portion of the poster or board.

Ask students to imagine themselves in the photograph and to write a new caption for the picture explaining how cleaning up the beach can help them feel like partners with God.

buttercups sweetened the early morning dew.

It was all good. And yet, something was missing. God wanted a creature who would enjoy the beauty and wonders of creation. God wanted someone—a partner—to watch over the world and take good care of it.

Caring Partners

Like Eve and Adam, we are all partners with God. Therefore, we too must watch over the world and take good care of it. How are these children working as partners with God? How can you?

So, the Torah tells us, on the sixth day God created Man and Woman. The man was called Adam and the woman was called Eve. They were God's finest creations.

28

Activity Suggestion

Bring a hardy plant to the classroom for the students to care for during the course of the year. Be sure to send it home with a student during vacation breaks.

Create a schedule so that each student has responsibility for the plant at some point during the year.

❖   ❖   ❖

The First Partners

Our sages taught that before God created Adam and Eve, God created the Garden of Eden. It was a most wonderful place. Ripe fruit hung plump and juicy from every tree and vine, and peacocks strutted their bright finery in the early morning sun. Goldfish swam in lakes filled with lily pads and sparkling blue water, and the hills and valleys were lush with grain and wildflowers.

When Adam and Eve were created, God said to them, "All that I have created, for you have I created it. If you do not keep it well, no one after you will be able to set it right."

29

Take a Closer Look

What would have happened to Adam and Eve if God had not taught them how to care for the garden?

As partners with God, we are given the responsibility of caring for the world. Create a bulletin board heading: "Caring for Our World." Ask students to bring in pictures that illustrate people taking care of God's world. Display the pictures on the board.

How to Teach the Story

The First Partners

Make sure students understand that this rabbinic story does not appear in the Bible.

Ask the students to describe a new skill they are learning this year (how to play a musical instrument, to dance, etc.). Who is instructing them?

Explain that in this story they will read how God teaches the first people—Adam and Eve—the skills they require to meet their own needs and to take care of the world.

Ask:

What kind of place did God give to Adam and Eve to live in?

Would you like to live in such a garden?

What happened to the garden? Did Adam and Eve understand what had happened?

If you were in their place, what would you think had happened to the garden?

What explanation did God give to Adam and Eve? How did they react? How would you have reacted?

Ask your students if they ever received a gift they knew was very precious, such as a family heirloom. Were they given special instructions about how to care for it? Did it make them feel extra special to be the recipient? Help the children see the analogy between this discussion and the story "The First Partners."

Ask the students to bring a picture from home of one of God's creations and have them explain how this creation has enhanced their lives.

To demonstrate that people are God's partners in Creation, bring oranges to class and continue the process of Creation by making orange juice (or make cucumbers into pickles).

Teach the Hebrew Lesson

The names of the five books in the Torah:

Genesis	בְּרֵאשִׁית
Exodus	שְׁמוֹת
Leviticus	וַיִּקְרָא
Numbers	בְּמִדְבַּר
Deuteronomy	דְּבָרִים

See page 11 in this guide for general suggestions for working with the Hebrew vocabulary words in the textbook.

At first Eve and Adam lived happily in Eden. Each day they explored its wonders and thanked God for the fruit of the vine, the peacocks' beauty, and the water that refreshed them.

But one day they woke up to find that the fruit was dry and filled with worms, the peacocks' feathers had lost their sheen, and all the plants were dying. Frightened, Eve and Adam prayed to God, "Creator of the Universe, please tell us why these terrible things have happened."

And God answered, "It is good that you enjoy all that I have made for you but you must learn to take care of it as well."

"Just show us what to do and we will do it," cried Adam and Eve. And so God taught them how to feed the peacocks and other animals, water and weed the fields, and plant new crops.

That is how Eve and Adam became the first farmers and the first partners with God.

❖ ❖ ❖

What All People Share

The Torah teaches us that Adam and Eve were the first people, the beginning of all families. This means that all people share one family story—the story of Creation. We also share one Creator—God, the Source of All Life.

HEBREW LESSON

Torah— תּוֹרָה
"Instruction"

Torah is the Hebrew name of the first five books of the Bible. The story of Creation is the very first story in the book of Genesis. Do you know the names of the other four books of the Torah?

30

A Note to the Teacher

A complete chapter in this book is devoted to the Torah. ("God's Teaching," Chapter 5). It is therefore sufficient for now to introduce only the Hebrew word *Torah* and the titles of the five books.

AND GOD CREATED...

The more we learn, the more we can appreciate God's wonderful creations. For example, the light of the sun is wonderfully bright. But did you know that it isn't really white? Sunlight is made up of all the colors of the rainbow.

A Hebrew poet who lived in Spain many, many years ago was amazed by God's creation of the sun.

He wrote:

"The sun has spread its wings over the earth
    to take away the darkness.
  Like a great tree, with its roots in heaven,
    and its branches reaching down to earth."

Can you write a poem about the sun?

31

If your synagogue has stained glass windows, try to find the opportunity to look at them with the light streaming through the colored glass.

Your students can make a stained glass window: Glue small pieces of torn or cut colored cellophane to a sheet of clear cellophane (10" x 10" square). Occasionally overlap the colored pieces to create new colors. Completely cover the clear cellophane. Glue strips of black construction paper to form additional designs. Cover the design with a second sheet of clear cellophane. Attach individual stained glass "panes" to the classroom window with cellophane tape to create a single large window effect.

**A Note to
the Teacher**

This poem was written by Judah Al-Harizi, a Hebrew poet who lived in Spain more than 250 years before Columbus.

SEARCHING FOR ANSWERS

When we study science, we learn how nature works. For example, we learn how water turns into ice and tadpoles into frogs.

When we study Torah, we learn how God cares for all living creatures. We also learn how the Jewish people made an agreement, or covenant, to work as partners with God to make the world a better place.

Read the questions below. Next to each one, write where you would search for the answer—in a science book (S) or in the Torah (T).

____**1.** Why do the Jewish people eat *matzah* on Passover?

____**2.** Why do runners eat bread and pasta before a race?

____**3.** How does a mother bird teach her young to fly?

____**4.** How does God teach us to care for one another?

____**5.** Who were the first astronauts?

____**6.** How can you become a good neighbor?

____**7.** How can you become a good scientist?

GOD'S CREATIONS

Of all God's creations, which is most important to you and why?

_____

_____

_____

_____

_____

_____

_____

_____

_____

_____

WORKING TOGETHER

Who plants a seed of corn?
Who causes the seed to sprout?
Who loosens the soil to help the plant grow?
Who causes the rain and sunshine to feed the plant?
Who harvests the ears of corn?

Who are the partners that make the corn?

_____

and

_____

Take a Closer Look

You might wish to elicit more examples of ways God and people work together on earth.

After studying this chapter, the student will understand:

1. We are all made in God's image.

2. By living as caring human beings, we remind each other of God's presence in the world.

3. God has given us the ability to distinguish good from evil and to understand right from wrong.

4. God expects us to act with respect toward others and to be responsible for our own actions.

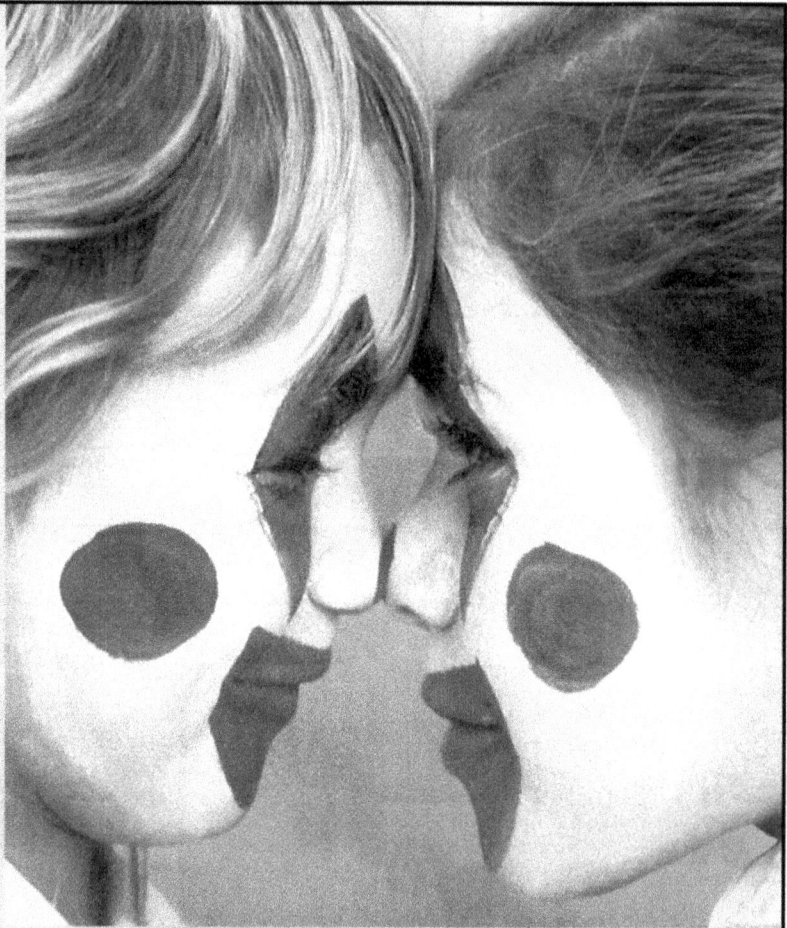

No two people look exactly the same—even when they try. But no matter how interesting, funny, beautiful, or handsome we look, it is how we act that matters most of all. How can we remind one another of God's presence in the world by the way we treat each other?

34

CHAPTER 4

In God's Image

D id anyone ever tell you, "You remind me so much of your mother"? Or, "You have your father's smile"? Or, "You're good in sports just like your aunt"?

When we have qualities in common with our relatives, the qualities are sometimes called

family resemblances. Some family resemblances are qualities that can be seen. For example, you may look like another family member. Other family resemblances are abilities people have in common, such as the ability to sing well or to make friends easily.

35

Hold up a mirror and ask a few students to look into it and describe what they see. Then ask them to look beyond their physical reflections and describe the character traits and qualities they have that are not reflected in the mirror's image.

Ask:

In what ways are you like other members of your family?

In what ways are you different?

Ask students to suggest words they might use to describe God. List them on the chalkboard. Then ask if any of these words can be used to describe people. Ask students what characteristics of God they can try to emulate, or develop themselves. Explain that being created in the image of God means we all have the potential to act in God-like ways.

From the Rabbi's Desk

When we teach children that they are created in God's image, we tell them something about their own uniqueness. It is not something they can measure. Nor is it a skill, such as the ability to speak, to understand, or even to love. It is the spark, the unique combination of qualities that makes them who they are. It is the soul they carry within.

We can give our students a sense of their own worthiness in many ways, but none is more important than reminding them that they are created in the image of God. Being created in God's image makes one invaluable, of infinite worth.

—DJW

Things to Talk About

People are more like one another than unlike one another. This is so because we all come from the one source of life, God. We are all members of one family—the human family.

When we say we are made in the image of God, we do not mean that we look like God, for we do not know what God looks like. Then what do we mean? What qualities might we have in common with God? For example, do we have gifts of wisdom and goodness that resemble, however faintly, the wisdom and goodness of God?

Ask students to tell about a time when their behavior made it clear that they were created in the image of God.

Tigers are terrified of fire, but despite their fear, they can be trained to jump through flaming hoops. Like other animals, tigers can follow orders and learn new tricks. But because they are animals, they cannot understand the difference between right and wrong. Because they were not created in God's image, animals cannot make choices that show respect for God's world.

Following in God's Ways

Because all people were created by God, we all share a certain family resemblance. It's not just that we all have feet, hands, and faces. It's something much more important.

You remember Adam and Eve. They were the first people. The Torah teaches that they were unlike any other creation because they were made in the image of God, *b'tzelem Elohim.* Like Eve and Adam, all people are made in God's image.

"But we look so different from one another," you say.

That's true. We do look different. To be created in God's image does not mean that people *look like* God or *look like* one another. It means that we are all born with the ability to follow in God's ways, to live as caring human beings.

For example, just as God shows concern for us by providing the warmth of the sun and the light of the moon, we can show our concern for others by sharing what we have and by offering our help to those in need.

36

Use the Photograph

Only people can make the choice to do good and not evil. Ask the students to share examples of situations they have been in when they had to make a moral choice. (Examples: They witness a child being mistreated by a group of students, or they have to explain to a teacher why a homework assignment is not done.)

Ask students to give examples of how animals are incapable of choosing right from wrong. (A cat will hunt a mouse and kill it in a slow and painful manner before eating it. Some fish will eat their young if they are not removed from the fish tank when they are born.)

Unlike computers, people can behave in ways that show respect for other people and appreciation for God's world.

When we speak, we can remember to speak with love. When we count money, we can remember to give *tzedakah*. And when we think, we can remember to praise God for all the good in our lives.

Only People Are Made in God's Image

Human beings are the only creatures made *b'tzelem Elohim.* Only people can understand the difference between right and wrong. Only people can make the choice between doing good and doing evil. And only people can treat themselves and God's other creations with respect. *All* people are partners with God.

What Makes People Different from Computers?

Computers are among the most extraordinary of human creations. Talented people have created these machines to work almost like the human brain. Computers can be programmed, or given instructions, to do many things— to talk, do math, and even think.

However, each of us is even more wonderful than the most extraordinary computer, for we are all created by God and in God's image. Unlike computers, we are not programmed by other people. We are responsible for our own actions. God has given us the ability to know right from wrong.

37

Ask your students why they think it is important to treat themselves with respect. (Since we are made in the image of God, it is our duty to treat ourselves with respect.)

What does respecting ourselves mean? do we show respect for ourselves when we skip meals? Don't get enough sleep? Overeat?

If we fail to care for ourselves, are we showing a lack of respect for God? Why?

Since we respect ourselves for being created in God's image, we must respect other people too. Is any one of us made "more" in the image of God than someone else? What are some of the ways in which we can honor God by showing our respect for others at home? In school? In our community?

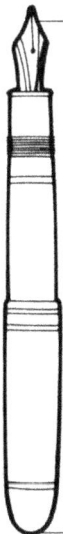

From the Rabbi's Desk

We must never let ourselves or our students forget that each and every one of us is created in God's image. This premise is the basis for all that follows. If we teach students that they are mere accidents of chemistry, or very clever animals, we cannot bring them a sense of sanctity and infinite worth. No matter how bad children may feel, you can reassure and comfort them that as a creation of God they have both a purpose and a capacity to be good and important. To be human is a glorious destiny.

—DJW

? Things to Talk About

How can you tell what a person is like on the inside? Children often find themselves in situations in which they need to make decisions about people, such as when they elect class officers and join clubs. List some of these situations on the chalkboard. With your students, discuss the fact that people are often attracted by a person's physical appearance or speech. Ask if these surface characteristics can be misleading. What about situations in which the surface characteristics are not those that are popularly considered attractive—a person who has a physical limitation or a speech impediment? Encourage your students to relate their personal experiences in this regard.

Use the Photograph

Ask each student to write a short essay or paragraph describing a time he or she provided assistance to someone. These can be illustrated and displayed under the heading, "We Are Made In God's Image."

Connecting with God Through Other People

Since all people are made *b'tzelem Elohim*, reaching out to others strengthens us and connects us with God. When we take on new responsibilities or challenges, we can work in partnership with others — teachers, friends, and family — and be strengthened by their help. When our assistance is needed, we can offer it graciously so that others may be strengthened by us.

> How do people learn right from wrong? What are some of the choices you can make that show you were created *b'tzelem Elohim?*

When you reach out to people and help them, you are following in God's ways. How can you help someone younger than you?

However, because we are human, we are not perfect. Even when we try our best, we sometimes make mistakes. When that happens, we can "get back on track" by doing our best to correct our mistakes and by offering our apologies to anyone we have hurt.

When others make mistakes, we can reach out to them by showing understanding and forgiveness.

By living as caring human beings, we remind each other of God's presence in the world and of the goodness of God's ways.

Jewish tradition suggests that there are 36 righteous heroes in every generation. These are people who have performed acts of goodness and justice for others. (Be sure to explain to your students that these people don't know that they are among the "36," nor does anyone else, and that these are not necessarily famous people.)

See if your class can come up with a list of people who might be counted among the righteous in this generation. Ask students what these people did to deserve a place on the list.

NATURE'S MIRROR

The river is like a mirror. You can see part of the city skyline reflected in it. Using the reflection as a guide, draw the buildings at the water's edge.

Because you were made *b'tzelem Elohim*, you are like a mirror that helps others see God's presence in the world. What can you do to reflect God's presence? How can your behavior guide others to follow in God's ways?

39

From the Rabbi's Desk

In our Jewish tradition, how we treat each other is even more important than how we treat God. God is all-powerful, but human beings are fragile. No *mitzvot* are more important than those that teach us to be tender with one another.

—DJW

Activity Suggestion

Since we are made *b'tzelem Elohim*, we must both learn and teach the difference between right and wrong. Ask your students to act out various situations in which they must learn or teach a rule of proper behavior. You might list a few ideas on the chalkboard to help spark their imaginations.

YOU BE THE TEACHER

Animals can be trained to follow orders. For example, a dog can be trained to sit quietly while the family is at the dinner table. However, a dog cannot *understand* that it is rude to interrupt people when they are eating. It cannot understand the difference between right and wrong, no matter how you try to explain it.

How would you train a dog to sit quietly while the family eats dinner?

_____

_____

Because people are made *b'tzelem Elohim*, they can understand the difference between right and wrong. In fact, people learn best when they are given an explanation of why it is right or wrong to behave in a certain way.

How would you teach a young child that it is impolite to interrupt someone who is speaking?

_____

_____

Did you recognize the city of Chicago reflected in the water on page 39?
This is how the skyline really looks.

40

REFLECTION

When you look in a mirror, you see your reflection.
When you hold writing up to a mirror, the words
appear backwards.
Can you read the message below?
(You can hold this page in front of a mirror to see how it looks.)

We were created
in God's image.
Our actions can
reflect God's ways

Write the message here:

_____

_____

List three things you can do this week to reflect that you were
created in the image of God.

I can _____

I can _____

I can _____

41

After studying this chapter, the student will understand:

1. God shows love for us by giving us rules or instructions for living. These rules and instructions are expressed in the Torah.

2. In order to understand God's instructions, we must study Torah.

3. The Torah keeps the Jewish people alive and strong.

4. The Torah contains stories of our ancestors and also has many commandments, or *mitzvot*. All of these help us to learn how God wants us to behave.

Imagine that someone gave you a game as a gift but when you opened the box there were no instructions inside. How would you know where to place the markers for each player, or when your turn came, or what was fair and what was cheating? It might be a great game but without the rules, how could you play it?

42

CHAPTER 5

God's Teaching

When we care about people, we want them to succeed and we try to give them what they need to be successful. Your parents care about you. They give you many things that help you grow and become strong—food, clothing, a warm house, and lots of love. They also set rules to keep you healthy and safe, rules that let you know when you must be ready for bed, how much TV you are permitted to watch, and where you are allowed to play.

Your teachers care about you too. They give you books, lessons, extra help, and even homework so that you will be successful in your studies. They also give you instructions to make sure you can do your best, instructions such as where to find a reference book, how to study for a test, and when to stop and ask for help.

43

How to Get Started

Ask the students how they would feel if their parents let them stay up as late as they liked. How would they feel if their parents *never* told them to go to bed? Ask them to imagine that their parents allowed them to do anything they wanted to do, at any time. Would they feel that their parents really cared about their well-being?

Do you think that parents and teachers who do not set rules or give instructions care more about their children or students? Why or why not?

From the Rabbi's Desk

Moral rules matter because they are greater than human invention: They are a Divine legacy. Moral rules *must* be Divine, for if they have their origin in human beings, then morality is only a matter of human opinion. One person may believe it is wrong to murder, another that it is right. On what basis shall we judge? But if God is the source of moral norms, *then* those norms have a solid, objective basis. A sense of objective right and wrong—of ethics and morality—is sorely needed in our world, and it is given to us by Judaism's insistence on one God who is passionately concerned about the righteousness of what we do.

—DJW

Discuss with students the purpose of rules and laws. Point out that people need laws to help them live in harmony with each other and to protect each other's rights.

How to Teach the Story

The Fox and the Fish

Ask students if they have ever felt pressured to do something that they didn't agree with. How did they respond?

Encourage students to discover for themselves the similarities between the fable of the fox and the fish and Rabbi Akiba's own situation with the Romans.

Do your students have an opinion or belief that is so important that they will stand by it even though others may think they are wrong?

According to the story, the fish would die when out of water, and the Jews would be in danger without study of Torah. Ask your students what they think would happen if Jews stopped studying Torah. Would we continue to exist as a people? What are some of the "foxes" that threaten to lure us out of the water? How should we react to them?

God Cares About Us

Because God cares about us, God gives us many gifts to help us live happy, healthy lives—food, air, rain, sunshine, and each other. God also gave us the Torah—the Five Books of Moses. The Torah teaches us how to live as creatures made *b'tzelem Elohim*, in God's image.

Being made in God's image is a precious gift and the Torah is the set of instructions that comes with that gift. In fact, the Hebrew word *Torah* means "instruction." In order to understand God's instructions, we must study Torah.

❖ ❖ ❖

The Fox and the Fish

Long, long ago, in the time of Rabbi Akiba, the Romans ruled the Land of Israel. The Romans wanted everyone to live exactly as *they* lived, and so they passed laws that made it difficult for Jews to practice their religion. One of these laws forbade the study of Torah, but Rabbi Akiba continued his studies.

One day a man came to Akiba and said, "Rabbi, do you know that you can be put to death for studying Torah?"

"Yes, I do," answered Akiba.

"Then why do you continue?" asked the man, his voice filled with disbelief.

"Let me tell you a story," said Rabbi Akiba. "Perhaps it will help you understand."

This is the story Akiba told:

Once, there was a sly old fox who was very hungry. He licked his chops and thought, "Fish are no match for a clever fox. I will catch my dinner in no time at all."

So the fox ran to the stream on the far side of the forest. Just then, an unsuspecting fish swam by.

"Oh, Miss Fish, I'm so glad to see you," said the sly old fox. "We must talk quickly for I fear for your life."

Alarmed, the fish swam closer to the shore.

"A group of fishermen are on their way, carrying long nets with which to catch you," the fox

44

A Note to the Teacher

It is important that your students understand that studying Torah is not like studying an academic subject like math or history. When we study Torah, we have an opportunity to hear God's "voice" and join with the generations of Jews who came before us. The Torah contains God's teaching, and as Jewish educators we have the job of instilling love of Torah in our students.

continued, lowering his voice so that the fish would come closer still. "We have little time. Let me help you out of the water and bring you to safety." And with that the fox slipped his paw into the water.

Just as the fox was about to grab the fish, she swam away, far beyond his reach. "Why do you swim away?" shouted the fox in surprise.

"I cannot leave the water," she called back. "For a fish out of water will surely die. But as long as I remain here, I have a good chance of escaping the fishermen's net and the paws of a sly old fox."

When Rabbi Akiba finished telling the story, he explained, "Just as fish need water to live, so the Jewish people need Torah. You see, even though it may be dangerous to continue studying Torah, we would be in much greater danger if we left our studies."

And with that, the rabbi smiled and went back to the study of Torah.

❖   ❖   ❖

45

Present the following, or similar situations that are meaningful to the students in your class. Have a pair of students act out the situation, developing various viewpoints.

Imagine you are on the committee for a school party and a suggestion is made to hold the party on a Jewish holiday. What would you do?

Imagine that a teenage friend invites you to go for a drive. You know he likes to speed, and you know your parents would not approve of your going with him. You say, "No thanks," and he answers, "Why, are you a baby?" What would you do?

Take a Closer Look

Help the class examine the different kinds of loyalties and allegiances in their lives. Try to expand the students' conception of what constitutes allegiance. For example, respecting parents, obeying the law, and getting along with friends are ways of showing loyalty.

Sometimes allegiances conflict. For example: your parents ask you to come straight home after school but your friends want you to play with them. Part of growing up means giving certain loyalties priority, deciding which are more important and which are less important. What sort of commitments must come first? Is there any one allegiance that stands above all others?

Ask the rabbi to permit the class to examine a *Sefer Torah* (Torah scroll). Perhaps the rabbi can talk with the class about the rules governing the writing and the reading of a Torah scroll.

Tour your synagogue sanctuary in order to examine some of the items depicted on these pages. If your synagogue has a particularly interesting artifact (perhaps a *Sefer Torah* rescued from the Holocaust or a *yad* brought from Europe by a congregant's relative), share the story and the ritual object with your students.

A TREE OF LIFE

Because the Torah helps keep the Jewish people alive, it is sometimes called *Etz Chayim*, or a Tree of Life.

Most synagogues have at least two Torah scrolls. The scrolls are kept in a cabinet called **Aron Ha-Kodesh**, or Holy Ark. When a *Sefer Torah* is taken out of or returned to the Ark, the congregation stands to show respect.

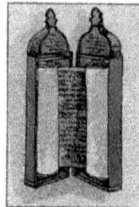

Sometimes the *Sefer Torah* is kept in a case made of wood decorated with leather or metal. The case opens up into two sections.

We show our love and respect by using beautiful coverings and ornaments to dress the Torah. A **mantle**, or coat, covers the scroll. A silver **breastplate** hangs over the mantle. And on the top there is often a *keter*, a crown.

A *ner tamid*, or eternal light, shines from the top of the Ark. Just as the *ner tamid* is always lit, so the Torah is like a source of light that is always there to guide us.

46

The Torah is written on a long scroll made of many pieces of **parchment**—about 250 of them—that are sewn together. The parchment scroll is attached to two wooden rollers. Each one is called an **Etz Chayim**, a "Tree of Life."

A **sofer**, or scribe, writes each **Sefer Torah** using a pen made from a feather, and black ink made from ground-up charcoal. It can take a full year for a scribe to complete one **Sefer Torah!**

The Torah is divided into weekly portions that are read aloud in the synagogue. Each portion is called **parashat ha-shavuah**. The person who reads the Torah portion uses a pointer called a **yad** ("hand").

Two silver ornaments with bells can also decorate the top of the Torah. They are called **rimmonim**.

During the service, people from the congregation are honored by being called up to the Torah when it is read. This honor is known as an **aliyah**. You will receive your first *aliyah* when you become a *Bat* or *Bar Mitzvah*.

47

Kindness to Animals
Tza'ar Ba'aley Chayim

The Torah records some of civilization's first laws for the prevention of cruelty to animals. In Jewish law even animals have rights. For example, it is forbidden to take a young bird from the nest without first sending away its mother (*Deut. 22:6*); to plow a field by yoking together two animals of different species, since the weaker or smaller of the pair would be made to suffer (*Deut. 22:10*); or to muzzle an animal while threshing so it cannot nibble the grain as it works (*Deut. 25:4*). Hunting for sport is prohibited. Not only does Judaism forbid cruelty to animals, it also demands kindness to them. For example, the Torah's law of Shabbat rest applies to domesticated animals as well as to people (*Exod. 20:10* and *Deut. 5:14*). The rabbis later added that people must feed their animals before they themselves sit down to eat.

Invite students to bring in photographs of their pets and display them on the bulletin board. Ask your students to describe the ways they help care for their pets and thus follow the teachings of the Bible.

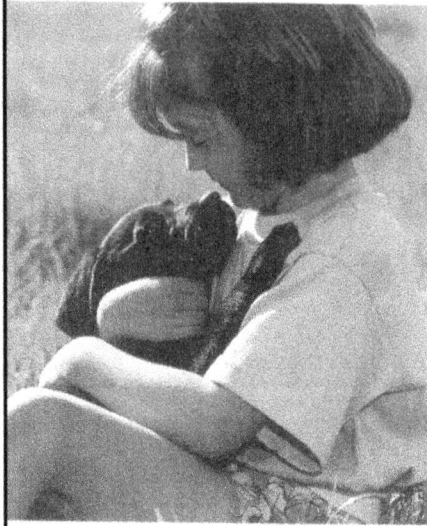

The Torah teaches us to show loving kindness to one another and to God's other creatures. Can you imagine what the world would be like if we were not taught to be kind and to treat one another with respect?

What Does the Torah Teach?

The Torah contains stories about God and our ancestors Abraham and Sarah, Rebecca and Isaac, Rachel, Leah, and Jacob, and many others. Their stories are the stories of our people and of our partnership with God. By studying what our ancestors did, we can learn how God wants us to behave.

"But they lived so long ago," you may say. "Their lives were very different from ours. What can we learn from people who lived back then?"

Many things. Just as Rebecca showed kindness by giving water to Abraham's camels, so we can show kindness by taking care of our pets —feeding them and cleaning their cages or taking them for walks. Just as Joseph forgave his brothers for treating him badly, so we can forgive friends or family who may sometimes be thoughtless or unkind. And just as Miriam

48

The Torah teaches us that to show disrespect for one of God's creations—a person, an animal, or the environment—shows disrespect to God. Do your students think this is so? Why or why not?

watched over her brother Moses, so we can show concern and respect for the people around us.

The Torah includes many commandments, or *mitzvot*, that help us understand what it means to be kind, forgiving, respectful, and unselfish. For example, the Ten Commandments are in the Torah. They tell us to honor our mothers and fathers, to remember Shabbat, and to be honest. The Torah also tells us to give charity, or *tzedakah*, to those in need and to treat others as we want to be treated by them.

When we study Torah, it is as if God is speaking to us, letting us know what is important and right, showing us how to be the best we can be.

What kind of person would you like to be? How can studying Torah help you become such a person?

HEBREW LESSON

Tzedakah "Charity" צְדָקָה

The Hebrew word *tzedakah* comes from the word *tzedek* which means "justice" or "righteousness." One way to be a just or righteous person is to give *tzedakah* to the needy.

49

Take a Closer Look

Why do some people have more than they need while others do not have nearly enough? In the Jewish viewpoint, a poor person is in a state of disinheritance. Charity is a way of restoring, in part, a person's *rightful* share of worldly goods. And so the Hebrew word for acts of charity and loving-kindness—*tzedakah*—also means righteousness or justice. The rabbis felt that if poverty existed, it was society that created it, and therefore society must right the wrong.

Even the poor are commanded to give *tzedakah*. Ask students why they think this is so.

Take a Closer Look

Ask your students what a goal is. Do they have goals for today? For next week? For this school year? What are they planning to do to reach their goals? Why is it important to pick the right goals for yourself? How can you tell when you've chosen the right goals? Must a goal be reached in order for it to be worthwhile? (Remind the class that "it is not our duty to complete the work, but neither are we free to desist from it." [*Pirke Avot 2:16*]. We live in a world of becoming, where perfection belongs only to God.)

Teach the Hebrew Lesson

When a new Hebrew vocabulary word is introduced, it is a good idea to take a few minutes to review the words that were previously covered. The new word can then be added to the Hebrew display in the classroom. This is also a good time for a quick Hebrew game or activity using the accumulated words. Examples of these activities are given on page 11 of this guide.

The root of the word *tzedakah* means "doing the right thing." Other common Hebrew words that use this same root are *tzedek* (justice), *tzodek* (correct), and *tzadik* (a righteous person). Discuss why these words share the same root. What common meanings do they share?

Have your students recreate the debate presented in "The Value of Study." Form two teams. Give them each a few minutes to gather their arguments. Then ask them to present their arguments in debate format.

TORAH DICTIONARY

These Hebrew words are often used when we talk about the *Sefer Torah.* Write a definition for each.

aliyah

_____

Aron Ha-Kodesh

_____

Etz Chayim

_____

keter

_____

ner tamid

_____

parashat ha-shavuah

_____

rimmonim

_____

sofer

_____

yad

_____

THE VALUE OF STUDY

A long time ago, two rabbis tried to decide which is more important—the study of Torah or living according to its laws.

Rabbi Tarfon thought it was more important to follow the laws of Torah. Rabbi Akiba argued that the only way to learn what the laws are is to study Torah.

In the end, the rabbis decided that studying Torah is more important when it leads to living according to the laws of the Torah.

You can learn to do many things by studying. List some by completing the sentences below.

By studying math, I can learn to

_____

By studying music, I can learn to

_____

By studying blessings, I can learn to

_____

By studying Torah, I can learn to

_____

50

IT'S A MITZVAH!

When we follow the commandments, or *mitzvot*, of the Torah, it is like tasting the fruits of the Tree of Life.

Read the list below. Then write each item that is a *mitzvah* in one of the fruits of the Tree of Life. Be prepared to discuss why it is a *mitzvah*. There is an extra fruit for you to write in an additional *mitzvah*.

- Light Ḥanukkah candles
- Visit an amusement park
- Visit a person who is ill
- Give *tzedakah*
- Help a parent
- Play video games
- Eat in a *sukkah*
- Forget your homework
- Study Torah
- Sing Shabbat songs

51

From the Rabbi's Desk

Goodness must be taught. For better or worse, unkindness and kindness are both natural to us in thought and in deed. Our children's religious and moral education is all about sorting out these tendencies.

In kindness, we please people and honor God. In cruelty, we hurt people and offend God. Children should learn early that goodness involves obligation. The Hebrew word *mitzvah* means not merely a good deed, but a commandment. Doing good brings God into this world as it enriches human beings.

—DJW

After studying this chapter, the student will understand:

1. Abraham was the first Jew to formulate the concept of one God.

2. Our ancestors taught us that God created the natural wonders and order in the world.

3. The *Shema* is an affirmation of Jewish belief in one God.

4. Sometimes we may stray from God and put our faith in false idols such as money or fame. We can always return to God, however, when we realize that only God is unchanging and forever.

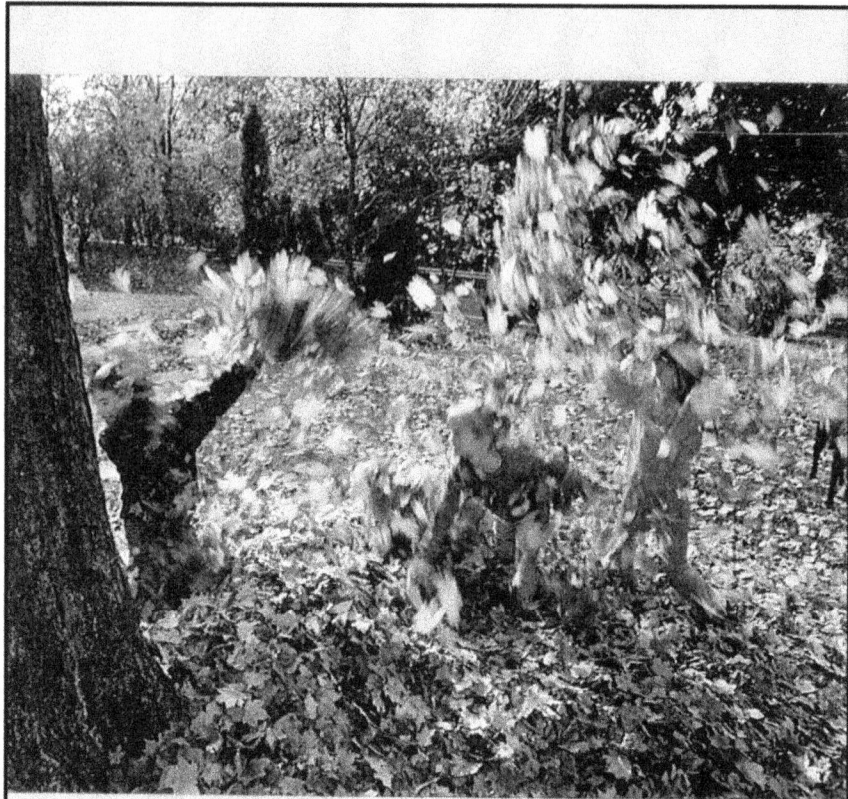

Each autumn the deep green of a trillion leaves turns into fiery shades of red, yellow, and orange. These changes let us know that the warmth of summer days will soon turn into the icy chill of winter. Yet we can enjoy the colorful swirl of autumn leaves because we understand that each season leads into another and returns in its time. We know that spring and summer will come again and the trees will blossom and bear fruit once more.

What do you enjoy most about autumn?

What do you look forward to as each September begins?

52

CHAPTER 6

God Is One

How would you feel if suddenly the sky were under your feet and the ground floated high above your head? Would you be afraid that you might fall through a cloud or that the ground might rain rocks instead of water drops?

Like the confidence we have that each season will come in its time, so our sureness of the ground under our feet and of the blue sky above helps us enjoy what we are doing. It feels good to know there is order in the world around us, to know that the sun will rise each morning and that the moon and stars will light the night sky.

53

How to Get Started

Lead a classroom discussion about the seasons of the year. Encourage your students to share what they like most about each season and what it might be like if one year their favorite season didn't arrive.

Help your students to see that the world is built on order. There are cycles of events that repeat in our lives over and over again. Can students name some events in their lives that create predictable cycles (holidays, losing teeth and growing new ones, etc.)? How does it feel to know that there are events that are certain to occur? What would life be like without order and predictability?

From the Rabbi's Desk

To ask a child a question is to open a door. Inside is a miscellany, filled with colorful bits, with fears and with fantasies. If we fail to ask the question, the door remains closed.

Encouraging children to ask questions, seeking to understand their worldview, trying to catch their wonder for the world—these can help in our own quest for God and can help train our students to look for God in their lives.

—DJW

When natural disasters such as hurricanes, earthquakes, and floods happen, it may feel as if all order has disappeared from the world. Though it is important to acknowledge this, it is also critical to recognize that the more scientists study, the more they uncover about the world's order, including the causes and warning signs of natural disasters. What scientists learn helps us plan ahead so that injuries and loss of life can be prevented when such disasters take place.

Activity Suggestion

During the winter months your students may feel gloomy about being in school when it is getting dark outside. But here's an opportunity to take advantage of the late afternoon hour and the sun's early setting.

On a clear late afternoon, bring your class outside to watch the sun set. Remind students about the order of God's creation of the world—day follows night and each day is a new creation.

Then ask the students to write a poem or draw a picture that expresses how they felt.

What Ancient People Believed

You have read how God created our world. When God looked at all the wonders and their order—the moon and stars in the sky above, and the green plants rooted in the earth below—God said it was good.

Long ago people did not believe that the wonders and order in the world were created by God. In ancient times people believed there were many gods that created the world. They believed that one god was in charge of the sun and another of the moon. They believed that other gods were in charge of the sea, the sky, and all the fish and fowl that live in them.

People made statues of clay and stone, called idols, to represent and honor their gods. The people prayed to the idols asking for their help. They also brought gifts to them hoping the gods would then cause rain to fall and water the fields, and cause the sun to shine so the crops would grow.

The Torah tells us that our ancestor Abraham was the first person to believe in one God. Although the Torah does not explain how Abraham came to

These idols are thousands of years old. Scientists called archaeologists dug them up. By studying the idols, we can learn about the beliefs of the people who made them.

54

From the Rabbi's Desk

Perhaps the greatest difference between polytheism and monotheism is this: Pagan gods cared only for how *they themselves* were treated. The God of Israel cares most for how human beings treat one another.

—DJW

believe in God, there are many legends that do. One legend, called a *midrash*, tells the story of how Abraham first came to believe in God when he was still a child.

❖   ❖   ❖

A *Midrash* About Abraham

While gazing up at the sky one day, young Abraham wondered, "Who created the heaven above and the earth below—and who created me?"

At first he was certain it was the sun. "Nothing is as powerful as the sun," thought Abraham. "Its heat warms all living things and its light shines throughout the world." And so Abraham spent the day praying to the sun, certain that *it* was the god of creation.

In the evening the sun set, slowly disappearing in the west as the moon rose in the east. Seeing this, Abraham said, "Forgive me, moon. *You* must be the creator of heaven and earth, the ruler of the universe. For surely the jewel-like stars that surround you are your crown."

And so Abraham stayed in the field all night praying to the moon, certain that *it* was the god of creation.

In the morning the moon sank in the west and the sun rose in the east once again. Seeing this, Abraham said, "Neither the sun nor the moon is great enough to create heaven and earth. And neither one created me. There is a greater power. That power is the one God—Creator of the sun, the moon, and the stars." And so Abraham prayed to the one God of all Creation.

❖   ❖   ❖

When the rabbis taught about God and explained the Torah, they sometimes created legends or stories, called *midrashim*. Some of these legends are as well known as the stories in the Bible. Each story, or *midrash*, teaches an important lesson. What did you learn from the *midrash* about Abraham?

A Note to the Teacher

Your students are being introduced to the basic difference between a polytheistic view of reality and a monotheistic one—a belief in many gods versus the belief in one God. It is crucial that they understand that this is not just a question of arithmetic (the belief in one versus the belief in many). Pagans saw life as controlled by a variety of forces, and often these forces seemed to conflict with each other. Pagans had no unified system or ideals to guide them.

Jewish history beings with Abraham's rejection of polytheism, and it proceeds with his quest for God.

Take a Closer Look

Share another midrash about Abraham with the class. Retell the story of Abraham and his father's idol shop as another example of Abraham's thoughtful quest for God. Ask students to compare the two stories. In what ways are they similar? What are some other examples of things we consider to have "power" but upon later examination find to be lacking it?

Abraham studied the world in search of truth. What does the example of his life teach us about the way we should live?

Ask students to speculate about who took the photograph, on what occasion, and for what purpose. Ask them to imagine themselves in the photograph and to write a new caption for the picture.

Things to Talk About

When the Israelites made the golden calf, they disobeyed God and Moses. They forgot that there is only one God. Later they realized their mistake and returned to God. Does the class think a person can make a mistake and fix it later? Ask students to give some examples of mistakes they have made and later corrected. Can they name famous people who had to correct mistakes publicly?

Just as our ancestors taught their children about God, Jewish parents continue to teach their children by sending them to religious school.

What the Torah Teaches Us

The Torah teaches us that Abraham and his wife Sarah were the first people to believe that God created the natural wonders and order in the world, and that it is God alone we must worship.

In the Torah, we read how Abraham and Sarah taught their son Isaac about God, how Isaac and his wife Rebecca taught their children, and how Jacob, Rachel and Leah taught their children. Soon there was an entire people —the Children of Israel—who believed in and worshiped God.

In the Torah we also learn that the Children of Israel sometimes strayed from their belief in God. While wandering in the wilderness after God freed them from slavery in Egypt, the Children of Israel became lonely and afraid. They made an idol of gold in the shape of a calf, and they prayed to it. They forgot that there is only one God. When they returned to their belief in God, they became strong again and were able to continue their journey to the Promised Land.

56

Hear O Israel

The *Shema* is very important. The words of the *Shema* appear in the Torah. They declare: Hear O Israel: Adonai is our God, Adonai is One.

שְׁמַע יִשְׂרָאֵל יְיָ אֱלֹהֵינוּ יְיָ אֶחָד.

Shema Yisrael Adonai Eloheinu Adonai Echad.

The *Shema* is said in a loud, clear voice during synagogue services. Some people recite the words of the *Shema* before they go to sleep at night. When you recite the *Shema*, you join other Jews in saying that you believe in the one and only God.

The *Shema* and one other section from the Torah are written on a parchment that is placed in a case. This case is hung on the doorposts of our homes. Together, the parchment and the case are called a *mezuzah*, which means "doorpost."

Mezuzah cases come in many sizes and shapes, but the parchment inside the case is the same in every *mezuzah*.

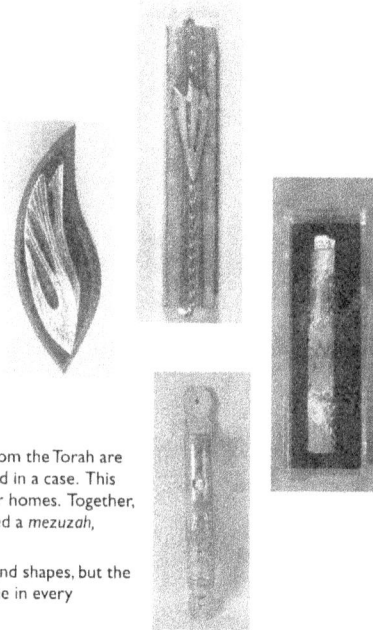

57

Give your students the opportunity to examine the parchment in a *mezuzah* case. Can they find the words of the *Shema*? Can they read them?

If your synagogue has a gift shop, visit it to look at the *mezuzot* sold there.

Teach the blessing recited when putting up a *mezuzah*.

Explain to the class that the six Hebrew words of the *Shema* are traditionally written with a large *ayin* in the word *shema* and a large *dalet* in the word *echad*. Together the *ayin* and the *dalet* spell the Hebrew word *ed*, which means "witness." This tells us that when we recite the *Shema*, we become witnesses to the oneness of God.

How to Teach the Story

The Window and the Mirror

Do we fully notice the people around us? Have your students close their eyes, and ask each to describe the classmate sitting beside him. What is she wearing? What is the color of her eyes? With their eyes still closed, have students describe what is outside the classroom window.

This story tells about a rich man who thinks only of himself. He is not an evil man but rather a foolish person who failed to do good deeds because he was unaware of the needs of those around him.

What is Mendel doing when the story begins? What kind of person is he?

Why does the rabbi come to Mendel's house?

After the rabbi leaves and Mendel looks out the window, what does he see? Had he been using the window as a mirror before the rabbi's visit?

How do you think Mendel will help his neighbors?

The Window and the Mirror

Mendel was the richest man in the village of Lem—and the stingiest! He loved money, and his greatest pleasure was counting it over and over and over again.

One day, Mendel sat counting his money for the fourth time since breakfast. He chuckled and smiled. The pile of silver coins in front of him was higher and brighter than any pile he had ever counted before.

Suddenly there was a knock on the door. Mendel quickly hid his money in an old metal box and opened the door. There stood the rabbi. Every Thursday he came by to ask for *tzedakah* to help the poor people of Lem buy food and candles for Shabbat.

Before the rabbi had a chance to speak, Mendel said, "I know that tomorrow night is erev Shabbat, and I know it is important for everyone to have candles, wine, and ḥallah. But rabbi, I cannot help everyone."

With that, Mendel reached into

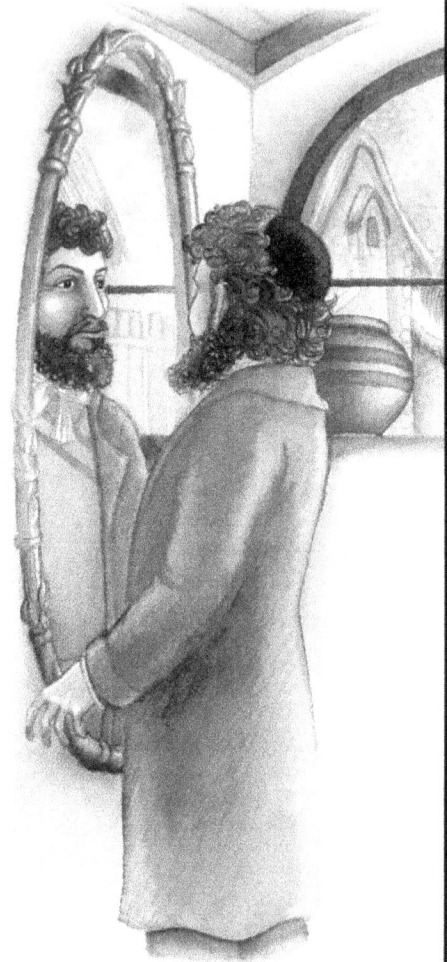

58

his pocket and handed the rabbi one small copper coin, just enough to buy a single candle. Expecting the rabbi to leave, Mendel walked toward the door. To his surprise, the rabbi remained where he was and pointed to the window.

"Tell me, Mendel," the rabbi asked, "what do you see when you look out the window?"

Mendel looked out. "I see the widow Rifka's house," he said.

"The paint is peeling, most of the windows are broken, and the garden is filled with stones and weeds."

Before turning away from the window, Mendel quickly added, "And, oh yes, I see a peddler selling potatoes."

Then the rabbi pointed to the mirror on the wall and said, "Now, Mendel, look in this mirror and tell me what you see."

"I see myself," Mendel replied.

59

Things to Talk About

What are some of today's false gods? Why do some people think that these things are more important than God?

Take a Closer Look

A mirror is glass coated with silver. It is like a window with its view blotted out. The silver that eliminates the view of the world is immediately understandable as representing money. (Note: The Hebrew word *kesef* means both "silver" and "money.") But it is equally important to develop the point that greed takes place in other than economic ways.

Encourage your students to see that miserliness is not the only form of greed. People can also withhold their love, their help, and themselves.

Would you like to have Mendel for your neighbor as he was at the beginning of the story? Would you like to live next door to him after he changed? Why?

Instead of using the mirror, if the rabbi had just told Mendel that he was behaving selfishly, do you think Mendel would have learned his lesson as well? Why or why not? How can stories teach us lessons?

Activity Suggestion

Have student(s) act out a person handling a mirror with self-respect, and then handling a mirror with self-love. What is the difference?

Allow students to scrape the coating from an inexpensive mirror to see how the glass changes.

"Isn't it interesting," the rabbi said, "both the window and the mirror are made of glass. The only difference is a thin layer of silver that lines the back of the mirror. Once you add a bit of silver, all you can see is yourself."

Mendel was relieved when the rabbi finally left. He very much wanted to count his money again. But the rabbi's words kept running through his head, "Once you add a bit of silver, all you can see is yourself."

Mendel looked out the window again. This time he saw the poor widow sweeping the street in front of her house. "Rifka looks so pale and weak," thought Mendel. "How can one person take care of seven children and such a big house? Why doesn't anyone help her?" he wondered.

Then he saw the peddler. This time Mendel recognized him. "Why that's Yankel," Mendel gasped. "He always helps me find my place in the prayerbook during Shabbat services. I didn't know he sold potatoes. He has eight children and his wife is ill. How can he support a large family on what a peddler earns? Why doesn't someone help him?"

The more Mendel looked out the window, the more people he saw—neighbors, friends, members of the community. For the first time in many years silver was not getting in the way. He was seeing other people and enjoying it—more than he enjoyed counting his money!

Mendel began to call out to the people he saw. He wished them a good day and a peaceful Shabbat.

Very soon Mendel realized that *he* could help those in need. And so he did. For now it gave him great pleasure to spend time with others and to live as a partner with God.

❖　　❖　　❖

60

Remembering What Is Important

Even today, people sometimes turn away from God and put their faith in false gods. Perhaps they doubt that God exists. Perhaps they become impatient because they doubt that God is powerful. Or perhaps they think we should put all our faith in science.

Today's false gods may not look like animals made of gold, and people may not even pray to them. But they are false gods all the same. Sometimes people forget about God and how important our partnership with God is. Instead they treat their possessions and money as if they were the most important thing. Or they treat themselves and what they want as if that was most important.

But money can be lost, fame can fade away, and expensive possessions can break. Only God is unchanging, forever and ever the First and the Last.

Enjoying the things we have is a healthy part of being human. But sometimes our possessions may become so important to us that we forget how precious friends and family are.

As partners with God, we must remember our responsibility to share what we have with others. How do you fulfill this responsibility?

61

Before completing the exercise on these pages, have the students brainstorm a list of *mitzvot* that they might draw upon during the week. List them on the chalkboard. You might want to place them in categories, such as things we do for God, things we do for ourselves, and things we do for others.

Activity Suggestion

WALKING WITH GOD

Do justice, love mercy, and walk humbly with Your God.

Micah

Give each student a sneaker cut from colored construction paper. In place of Nike or Reebok or Keds, have them write their own names on the heel. Then ask them to write on it something they do to show that they are partners with God.

Create a large "path" on the bulletin board and ask the students to attach their sneakers.

THE ROAD OF TORAH: *Derech Torah*

As you know, the Torah is the set of instructions on how to live each day as a creature made *b'tzelem Elohim*, in the image of God. The Torah teaches us to follow in God's ways by doing *mitzvot*. Each *mitzvah* gives us an opportunity to be the best people we can be. Each *mitzvah* reminds us that we are partners with God.

There are many *mitzvot*. Some help us celebrate Shabbat and holidays. Some help us show kindness and respect for ourselves and for God's other creations. And some teach us to praise God for the good in our lives.

When you do *mitzvot*, you join generations of our people on the Road of Torah, *Derech Torah*. Record some of the *mitzvot* you do this week. Try to write at least two for each day.

SUNDAY

Did you send a card to someone who is sick?

TUESDAY

MONDAY

Did you exercise your body today?

Did you help someone today?

62

THURSDAY

Did you
study Torah
today?

FRIDAY

SHABBAT

Did you
show
respect for
yourself
today?

Did you
recite the
blessing
over bread
today?

WEDNESDAY

Did you
water a
plant
today?

63

Understanding God's Ways

You have already discovered much about God's world and the wisdom of our tradition. How does being a partner with God make you feel? How can you work as a partner with other people to care for God's world?

Your search for answers and understanding about God will last for many years—until you are very old and your hair turns as white as snow. Over time, some of your ideas may change and some may stay the same. Throughout your life you will have many opportunities to share the answers you have found and the questions that remain.

For now, it is time to continue searching for more answers to your questions, such as "Does God hear our prayers?" "How can we know right from wrong?" and "Does God forgive us when we make mistakes?"

As you search for answers, your understanding of God's ways and of our people's tradition will grow. As you read the next chapters of *Partners with God*, you will learn how to listen to the gentle voice of your soul and how to reach the Island in Time that God creates for us each week. You will learn the many ways Jews speak to God and how our faith makes us strong.

Come, let us continue our search together. Let us share what we learn and celebrate our partnership with God.

65

Kaleidoscope

Bring a kaleidoscope (more than one, if possible) to class. Let the students look through it. (A kaleidoscope contains loose fragments of colored glass between two flat plates and two mirrors placed at 60 degree angles. When the position of the fragments is changed, the glass appears in an endless variety of forms.)

Discuss how learning about God is like looking through a kaleidoscope.

After studying this chapter, the student will understand:

1. Life is a miracle.
2. All life is holy.
3. Every creature in God's world has something to contribute.
4. God's wonders and miracles remind us of God's hidden presence in the world.

The universe is made up of billions of star systems. Each system is called a galaxy. Our sun is a single star in the Milky Way galaxy.

This is a photograph of Andromeda—the galaxy nearest to the Milky Way. It contains more than 300 billion stars. If you were to count Andromeda's stars, one star each second, it would take you more than 9,000 years to count them all!

What amazes you most about the universe?

66

CHAPTER 7

God's Wonders

Do you ever wonder what makes the sun set in the evening and rise in the morning? How, every month, the moon turns itself from a silvery sliver of light into a radiant full moon? And how billions of twinkling stars can move across the sky so silently when 20 sixth-graders can't go from the classroom to the playground without making a big commotion?

A great scientist, Albert Einstein, knew the answers to all these questions. He also understood why the sky is blue and the grass is green, how birds fly and fish breathe, and why raindrops plop *down* and plants shoot *up*. And even though he understood this—and much, much more—Albert Einstein believed that all life is a miracle.

67

From the Rabbi's Desk

Religion asks those who see the world as workers to see it anew as artists. Noticing what is wonderful and allowing it to seep into our consciousness is the beginning of cultivating a sense of wonder. To understand the artist, one must take notice of the work of art. One way of finding God is to join together with our children in appreciating the artistry of the world.

—DJW

How to Get Started

Ask students to name things in nature that occur every day or often (the sun rises and sets, the moon appears in the night sky, etc.). Then ask them to imagine the world without any of these things. What would the world be like?

Take a Closer Look

Write the names of some of God's creations on index cards, one on each, and pin one card on the back of each student. Invite students to go around the classroom asking questions of one another that can be answered "yes" or "no" to discover the name of the creation written on their backs.

A Note to the Teacher

Albert Einstein was a Jew who deeply cared about all people. He received many honors in his lifetime including the Nobel Prize. In 1952 he was asked to become president of the State of Israel. Although he refused the honor, his support of Israel remains an important contribution to our people's history.

Take a Closer Look

The First Telegram

Tell the students that in the days before computers and fax machines, a telegraph was used to send telegrams, an early form of electronic mail. The telegraph was invented by Samuel F. B. Morse. On May 24, 1844, the first telegram ever sent went from Washington to Baltimore. It was an exciting event. The telegram quoted a verse from the Bible: "What hath God wrought!" (What has God made!) (*Numbers 23:23*)

Ask:

Since it was a person who invented the telegraph, what do you think the message meant?

Use the Photograph

Help your students see that when we appeal to magic to solve our problems for us, we relinquish control over our lives and thereby deny the knowledge and skills God has given us.

Life's Wonders and Miracles

Are you surprised that a scientist who knew so much thought that life is a miracle?

Like many other wise people, Albert Einstein believed that the beauty of nature, the goodness of people, and the adventure of learning are all part of life's daily wonders and miracles. He believed that behind every mystery he uncovered, there was yet another mystery he could not solve. He believed that as much as science can explain, there is even more it *cannot* explain.

Throughout history people have tried to understand the source of life's mysteries and wonders. The Jewish people believe that God is the source. That is why we praise God in our prayers.

Once we know how the magician pulls the rabbit from a hat, we understand the trick and there is no mystery. But the more science teaches us about our universe, the more we are filled with the wonder of God's presence.

What is a "miracle"? Is it magic? Is it something that science can explain, but still seems very special? Or is a miracle something that science cannot yet explain?

Name three things you think are miracles.

From the Rabbi's Desk

Albert Einstein said, "There are two ways to see the world. One is to see nothing as a miracle. The other is to see everything as a miracle." Since it is wondrous that *anything* exists, the lesson is clear: we are surrounded by marvels each day.

—DJW

❖　　❖　　❖

David and the Spider

Some years before David became King of Israel, he sat in his garden enjoying the shade of a pomegranate tree and the sweet fragrance of its blossoms. As he admired the branches that fanned out above him, he noticed a spider weaving a lacy web between two twigs.

Annoyed by this uninvited guest, David asked God, "Creator of the Universe, why did You bring such a useless creature into the world? What good does it do?"

God answered, "Do not look down on this creature. One day you will thank Me for creating spiders and understand how precious and extraordinary *all* Creation is."

Time passed and David was no longer sitting comfortably in his garden. His friend Jonathan— King Saul's son—had warned him that his life was in danger and that he must run away. "My father is jealous of you," Jonathan said with concern in his voice. "He is afraid the people will make

69

David and the Spider

When David was about 20 years old, he was invited to join King Saul's court, to try with harp and his sweet voice to dispel the old king's sadness. Jonathan, Saul's son, became his closest friend. King Saul became very jealous of David and finally he was forced to flee.

Ask students if they can think of creatures the world would be better off without. List them on the chalkboard.

After reading the story, see if the class can think of worthwhile purposes that the listed "dispensable" creatures might serve.

Activity Suggestion

When children can see familiar things in a new way, they can better understand God's presence in our world.

Ask students to look at a leaf, a flower, etc. Then allow them to examine it using a magnifying glass. Ask them to describe something about the object that they didn't see before.

you King of Israel in his place. You must escape now before his soldiers come and kill you."

And so David fled. Moving as fast as he could, he hid in forests and mountains. Each time Saul's soldiers came closer, David had to move on.

Months passed and David became weak and exhausted. "How much longer can I run and hide?" he wondered. But fearing for his life, David kept running further and further away.

Finally, he came to the wilderness of Ein Gedi. David looked around. The only place to hide was in a small cave. Having no choice, he went inside.

The cave was quiet and still. At first, all David could hear was the loud thumping of his heart. Then suddenly, there was a great noise outside. King Saul's soldiers had arrived and were standing at the entrance to the cave.

"They will surely find me," David thought, his heart beating more loudly than before. "What can I do? There is no way for me to escape!"

David listened carefully, waiting for the king's men to enter the cave. But they did not.

"He's nowhere to be seen," one of them called out.

"No point in searching this cave," said another. "There's a huge spider's web across the entrance. If David were here, he would have broken it as he went in." And with that, the soldiers left.

David could not believe his ears. He walked toward the entrance of the cave. Sure enough, a spider had saved his life by spinning a web across the mouth of the cave. David marveled at how extraordinary the spider was. Her delicate web had protected him better than any wall of stone or iron.

As David left the cave, he said to the spider, "Blessed be your Creator and blessed be you. For all life is holy and all Creation is a miracle."

❖   ❖   ❖

Science can explain many of the whys and hows of nature, but it cannot explain what came before nature or why the world was created. The Jewish people believe that God came before nature and that God gave us the Torah so that we could understand the purpose of Creation.

Some people think earthworms are so ugly and slimy they want to step on them. But here are a few facts you should know:

The holes earthworms dig let air into the soil which keeps the soil fresh.
The holes let water into the soil which helps plants grow.
The holes also make spaces for tender plant roots to grow freely.

Now that you know this, would you step on an earthworm?

71

Take a Closer Look

Every creature in God's world has something of value to contribute, although it may be difficult for us to recognize what it is.

Do your students agree?

Can any of them think of any animal or insect with nothing of value to contribute? Does anyone else disagree and find something of value about this creature? (If the class concludes that a given animal—a rat or a snake perhaps—has no redeeming value, one of the children might do some research to find out whether, in its natural habitat, the creature does in fact contribute in some way to the order and/or beauty of creation.)

A Note to the Teacher

This would be a good time to pause and address some of the specific questions students have. Ask students to write their questions on paper. Then you can give the questions to the rabbi and invite the rabbi to visit the class to answer some of them.

Even though God is hidden, we can feel God's presence. Ask students to think of times they felt God's presence and describe what they were doing.

Discuss the places or situations that can help us to feel God's presence.

God's Wisdom Is a Mystery

To live as a Jew is to feel the wondrous love and wisdom of God, hidden—like a mystery—in all things. Hidden in the silence of a starry night, the syrupy sweetness of honey on Rosh Hashanah, and even in the delicate weave of a spider's web.

What wonders remind *you* most of God's hidden presence? What fills you with so much good feeling that you want to jump for joy? The excitement of a touchdown? The sound of the High Holiday *shofar?* The gentle flutter of a butterfly?

Have you felt God's hidden presence as you watched a trapeze artist soaring high above the circus crowd? Are you moved to amazement by the extraordinary animals in the zoo—floppy-eared elephants as big as a house and furry seals that wriggle and jiggle their bodies about?

Does the crash of thunder or the blaze of lightning streaking across

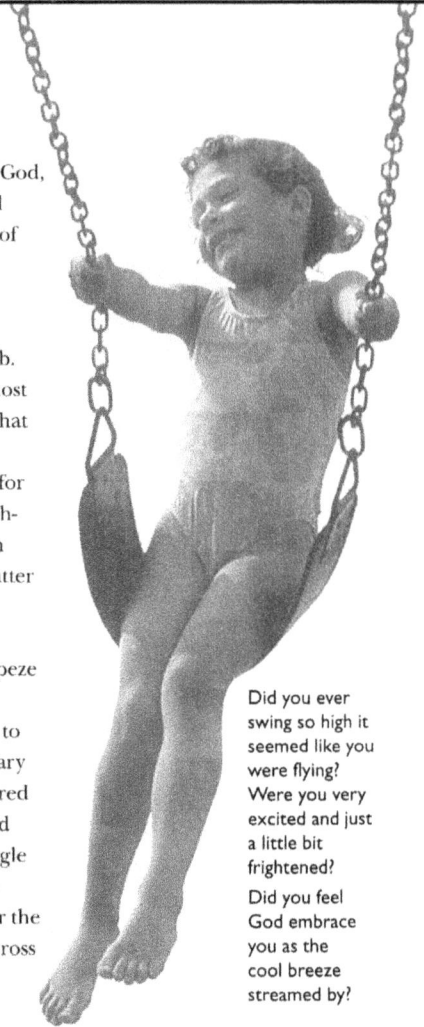

Did you ever swing so high it seemed like you were flying? Were you very excited and just a little bit frightened?

Did you feel God embrace you as the cool breeze streamed by?

72

the sky fill you with awe and wonder? What do you feel as the *Sefer Torah*—dressed in smooth velvet and wearing a gleaming silver crown—is carried past you in the synagogue?

Our sages saw mysteries and miracles in each of God's creations. They praised God by chanting, "Blessed are You, Adonai our God, Ruler of the universe, who brought such wonders into the world."

When you are filled with joy and wonder, you too may want to recite this *brachah*.

Activity Suggestion

Bring a glass of water and packets of sugar to class (don't let the students see the sugar).

Ask students to observe and describe the glass of water on your desk. Ask a student to take a sip and to describe the taste. Ask that same student to step outside the classroom for a moment, add sugar to the water, stir it until it is completely dissolved (powdered sugar substitute dissolves more easily). Then invite the student to return and taste and describe the water once again.

Explain that you added sugar (although the student cannot see it) and the water became sweet even though it looks the same as it did before.

In the same way, although we cannot see God, our awareness of God's presence makes our lives "sweeter."

IT'S AMAZING!

The human body is one of the greatest miracles in God's world.

It is estimated that your brain can store 100,000,000 pieces of information in a lifetime.

What are the three most amazing pieces of information you know?

_____

_____

_____

_____

_____

_____

Your heart weighs less than one pound, yet it does enough work in one hour to lift a weight of 3,000 pounds more than a foot off the ground. Your heart is linked by 100,000 miles of pipelines—veins and arteries—to all parts of your body, and it beats more than 700,000 times from one Shabbat to the next.

About how many times does your heart beat in one month? _____ **In one year?**_____

What do you find most amazing about the human body?

_____

_____

_____

_____

_____

_____

74

LET US PRAISE GOD

The morning prayer service contains songs of praise to God, *Pesukei De-Zimra*. Here are several lines from one song. Can you underline the words that tell how we can praise God?

Give thanks to God, call out God's name,
Let all people know of God's great deeds.

Praise God in song and music,
Remember all God's wonders.

Celebrate God's holy name,
May the hearts of those who seek God rejoice.

Remember the wonders God has made,
God's marvels and justice.

WRITE A SONG OF WONDER

Songs, or *z'mirot*, are an important part of the Jewish tradition. We sing many of our blessings and prayers, and we welcome Shabbat and holidays with songs. Music can help us express our feelings of delight and wonder.

Can you write a song about the wonders in your life? As you write the words on the lines below, think about the music. You can make up your own or use the melody of a song you already know.

75

After studying this chapter, the student will understand:

1. Even though all human beings have many things in common, each person is unique.

2. Each person has a soul. Our souls connect us to each other, and to God.

3. Our souls help us to know right from wrong, to live as creatures made *b'tzelem Elohim*, to see good in others, and to use our talents for good. Our souls move us toward Torah.

4. The body and the soul form a partnership to help us live as creatures made *b'tzelem Elohim*. We must learn to care for both.

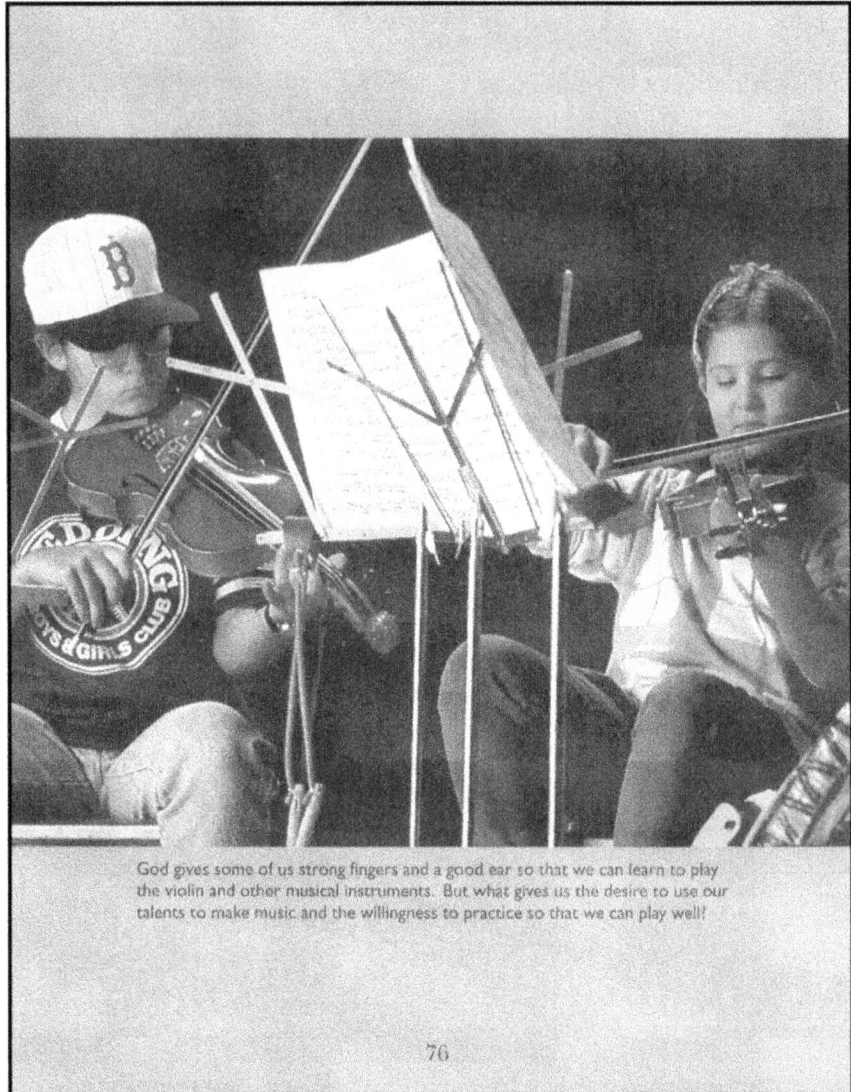

God gives some of us strong fingers and a good ear so that we can learn to play the violin and other musical instruments. But what gives us the desire to use our talents to make music and the willingness to practice so that we can play well?

76

CHAPTER 8

Listening to Our Souls

Are there times when you wish you could be someone else? Someone you think is smarter, better looking, or more popular than you? Someone you are convinced is more talented or more special than you? If you have, it's a shame, because *you* are quite special. In fact, no one else is exactly like you.

77

How to Get Started

Ask the students if they know people who try to pretend they are somebody else, or who try to pretend they are not what they really are. Are such people happy individuals? Why do they think so?

Everyone is special. Consider going around the class and naming one special characteristic of each student in the room. Or, ask students to express a special characteristic of one of their classmates.

From the Rabbi's Desk

When children do something wrong, they often know it instinctively, even if they cannot put their finger on what was wrong about what they did. When children do something right—when they perform a mitzvah—the same thing often happens. And the sense children get when they are useful, when they can understand the mitzvah and actually do it, lifts their souls.

—DJW

Every species of animal has some particular characteristic that helps it survive—sharp claws, great speed, a thick hide, and so forth. What characteristic is unique to human beings?

Activity Suggestion

Using water-based ink pads—they are available in different colors—have each child make a fingerprint on a piece of paper.

Explain to students that each of our fingerprints is unique—different from anyone else's. In the same way, God creates no two people exactly alike. Each one of us is special.

Now ask students to make their print(s) into a picture, e.g., fingerprints can become red flower petals or green leaves on a tree; a single print can be turned into a bee by adding stripes and wings, or into a face by adding eyes, nose, and mouth. You'll probably be pleasantly surprised by how inventive and creative your students can be. *(Be sure to use washable water-based ink pads!)*

Many animals are delightful and some are among the great wonders of our world. But only people are made *b'tzelem Elohim* and only people have souls.

You Are Special

Of course, you have a great deal in common with other people. For example, like other people you were made *b'tzelem Elohim*, in God's image. Like other people you need air, food, and water. And like other people you cry when you are hurt and laugh when you hear a good joke.

Even though a list of all the ways in which you are like other people would be very long, there is still much about you that is special and wonderful in the way that only you can be special and wonderful. This is so because you have a personality that is yours alone and a soul of your own—a precious gift from God.

78

What the Torah Teaches

The Torah tells us that God created the first person—Adam—from dust and then blew the breath of life, a *neshamah*, into him so that he might become a human being. And so it has been since Creation that at birth every person receives a *neshamah* from God. You received one when you were born. It is your personal connection with God, a divine spark of holiness that glows inside you and that will last for all time.

The Torah teaches that our souls are also our special connection with one another. For, just as all people were created *b'tzelem Elohim*, all people—rich and poor, young and old, Jew and non-Jew—have souls, a spark of God that glows inside them.

Just as birds are certain of the direction in which they must fly—south for the winter and north in the spring—our souls guide us in the direction of Torah. And just as birds know north from south, our souls know right from wrong.

A Note to the Teacher

Children are very concerned about how well they measure up to their peers. Our society is highly competitive, and children are often evaluated and categorized according to their skills and scholastic achievements. Compounding the problem, the media frequently present idealized pictures of people. Children can be misled into feeling inferior if they do not seem to be as talented as actors in a commercial, or if they cannot solve their problems as easily as the smiling characters of a television family.

As the teacher, you can counteract these effects. When you are willing to accept each member of the class as a worthwhile individual, you help develop in your students the all-important sense of self-esteem. You encourage them to explore the potentials of what they might hope to become.

Teach the Hebrew Lesson

The concept of a soul is very important to the Jewish people. We can see this importance reflected in the Hebrew language. There are three different Hebrew words to express the concept of soul. In this book we use the word *neshamah*; the other two words are *ruach* (also used for wind) and *nefesh*. Ask students why they think we use so many different words to express the idea of a "soul"?

Activity Suggestion

Give each student a card with five blank lines, each followed by "ing."

_____ ing

_____ ing

etc.

Have students fill in the card with words that they believe describe themselves. For example: growing, loving, fighting, etc.

Take a Closer Look

How can people show they are created in the image of God by the way they undertake and complete their daily work?

Ask students to name different kinds of occupations and professions (letter carrier, doctor, teacher, carpenter, accountant, nurse, sanitation worker, etc.). List them on the chalkboard.

Discuss how each one can show that he or she is created *b'tzelem Elohim*—in God's image—by the way the work is done.

How Our Souls Influence Us

Although our souls cannot be seen, they are real. Just as our personalities are invisible yet stand out, so too our souls are an important ingredient in who we are and what we do. They help us know right from wrong, live as creatures made *b'tzelem Elohim*, see the good in others, and use the talents we have to the best of our ability.

A person with a good sense of humor may enjoy telling jokes. A person who is shy may enjoy spending time alone. How would you describe your personality? How does it influence what you do?

One way we know that people have souls is by observing their actions. When someone behaves as a creature made *b'tzelem Elohim*, we are reminded that the person has a soul, a connection with God. When people are kind, honest, and loving, we often feel touched by the goodness of their souls. What do people do that reminds you they have souls? What do you do because you have a *neshamah*?

❖　　❖　　❖

Who Will Be Zusya?

Once there was a rabbi named Zusya who loved God with all his heart and soul, and who treated all God's creatures with respect and kindness.

Rabbi Zusya studied Torah, kept Shabbat, visited the sick, and praised God for all the goodness in the world. Though he was not a rich man, Zusya gave generously to those in need. Students came from far and near, hoping to learn from this gentle and wise rabbi.

Zusya often told his students, "Listen to the still, small voice inside you. Your *neshamah* will tell you how you must live and what you must do."

Each day Rabbi Zusya's students came to the House of Study, called the *Bet Midrash*, eager to learn what they could from him.

80

One day, Zusya did not appear at the usual hour. His students waited all morning and through the afternoon. But Zusya did not come. By evening his students realized that something terrible must have happened. So they all rushed to Zusya's house.

The students knocked on the door. No one answered. They knocked more loudly and peered through the frost-covered windows. Finally, they heard a weak voice say, "*Shalom aleichem*, peace be with you. Come in."

The students entered Rabbi Zusya's house. In the far corner of the room they saw the old rabbi lying huddled in bed, too ill to get up and greet them.

"Rabbi Zusya!" his students cried. "What has happened? How can we help you?"

"There is nothing you can do," answered Zusya. "I am dying and I am very frightened."

"Why are you afraid?" the youngest student asked. "Didn't

81

Who Will Be Zusya?

This story is about a rabbi who lived almost 200 years ago in Eastern Europe. Many stories are told about Rabbi Zusya—in particular, how he taught others by the example of his own life. In the story we will see how Rabbi Zusya, even while dying, taught his students a valuable lesson.

What kind of person was Rabbi Zusya?

How did Zusya's students feel about him?

How did they know that something must be wrong with Zusya?

Why was Zusya afraid? (Do you think he was really afraid, or was he trying to teach his students something?)

What did Zusya teach his students about how they should live their own lives?

Do you think God will judge Zusya favorably? Why?

Are there people in your life whom you respect and love as Zusya's students loved him? Who? Why?

you teach us that *all* living things die?"

"Of course, every living thing must die some day," said the rabbi.

The young student tried to comfort Rabbi Zusya, saying "Then why are you afraid? You have led such a good life. You have believed in God with a faith as strong as Abraham's. And you have followed the commandments as carefully as Moses."

"Thank you. But this is not why I am afraid," explained the rabbi. "For if God should ask me why I did not act like Abraham, I can say that I was not Abraham. And if God asks why I did not act like Rebecca or Moses, I can also say that I was not Moses."

Then the rabbi said, "But if God should ask me to account for the times when I did not act like Zusya, what shall I say then?"

Do you think anyone succeeds in being her or his own best self 100% of the time? Does it help to try? How can you try to be your best self?

The students were silent, for they understood Zusya's final lesson. To do your best is to be yourself, to hear and follow the still, small voice of your own *neshamah.*

❖   ❖   ❖

82

How Our Souls Guide Us

Have you ever felt something deep down inside move you to hug someone who was sad or to help a hungry or injured animal? Was the feeling like a quiet voice in your head or a gentle tug in your heart? Do you think it might have been your soul guiding you to show loving kindness to another of God's creatures?

It is said that our eyes are like windows from which our souls look out and see the world. Through our eyes, our souls can see the many opportunities to do good—to be helpful, kind, and honest. But when we ignore the opportunities to do good or when we do things we know are wrong, such as being selfish, mean, or dishonest, it is as if we bring our eyelids down like shades and blind our souls.

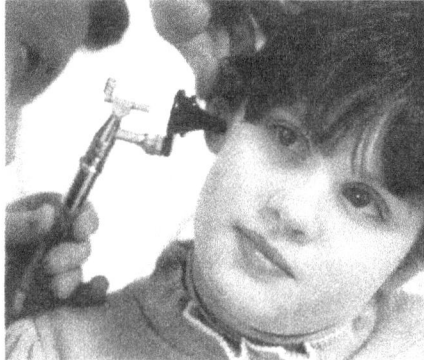

Taking Care of Your *Neshamah*

When your soul guides the actions of your body, it works in partnership with your body to help you live as a creature made

One way we take care of our bodies is by going to the doctor for regular check-ups. Do you think we can take care of our souls? How?

83

Things to Talk About

Ask your students to imagine a situation in which what their souls tell them conflicts with acceptance by others. Help the class figure a way to resolve the conflict. For example, a group of your friends want you to join them in a prank—throwing snowballs at a passerby. You know it is wrong, but you don't want to be a spoilsport. Is being part of the group for a short while more important to you than being kind to others? Suppose you refuse to go along with the prank? Your friends might be angry with you for a time, but will they later come to respect you for your convictions? In the long run, do you think your friends will come to value your friendship more? If not, do you think these are the kinds of friends you really want?

From the Rabbi's Desk

When we are young, we learn to do many things by rote, even though we may not always see the value in them. Gradually we come to appreciate good behavior for its own sake. The same hope holds with goodness. We teach it in the hope that children not only will come to *do* good but will come to *understand* its importance.

—DJW

Give students lined paper (one sheet per pupil) and ask them to fold the sheets in half lengthwise to form two columns. On the left column, have students complete the following sentences (or others similar to them):

I would like to learn to . . .

I would like to get along better with people by . . .

I would like to love my parents better by . . .

Tell students to skip five or six lines between each statement.

On the right column, next to each statement, have the student list the first steps they could take to achieve each goal.

b'tzelem Elohim. Therefore, to do your very best, you must take care of both your body *and* your soul.

In what ways do you take care of your body? How about your soul? Do you think it's possible to care for something you cannot see?

It may be easier than you think. In the same way you strengthen your body with healthful foods, so you can nourish your soul with the wisdom of Torah. Just as you exercise your body by running and playing sports, so you can exercise your soul by performing *mitzvot*. And just as you have regular check-ups with your doctor, so you can

check in regularly with God by saying blessings and other prayers.

Pay attention in the morning as you take your first waking breath. You may feel the spark of God light up, silently filling you with its mystery and music. And then you can say the words Jews have said for generations: "I thank You everlasting Ruler who has restored my soul to me in mercy. Great is your faithfulness."

Your *neshamah* can help you see the good in others. When you listen to that quiet voice inside you, it can help you choose caring and kind friends.

84

**Take a
Closer Look**

The prayer above is *Modeh Ani*. (You might like to have the students locate the prayer in the *siddur*.) It is recited upon waking in the morning. Discuss the meaning of the prayer. Does the moment we open our eyes in the morning seem like a good time to pray? Why or why not? Why might we talk to God about our souls at this time of the day?

EXERCISE YOUR NESHAMAH

When you climb a tree, you exercise your body. Here are some ideas of how you can use a tree to exercise your soul.

- Sit in its shade and read a book.
- Paint a picture of it.
- Show your appreciation for trees by celebrating the holiday of Tu B'Shevat.

Can you think of other ways to exercise your *neshamah* by appreciating nature?

_____

_____

_____

_____

_____

_____

_____

_____

_____

_____

_____

_____

_____

85

We exercise our souls when we do *mitzvot*. What are some *mitzvot* we might do on a regular basis to help keep our souls healthy? You might like to create a chart or poster of these to hang in the classroom.

Each *mitzvah* we do not only exercises our souls, but also brings us closer to God. The Kabbalist said we are all connected to God by a thin thread of holy light, and when we do *mitzvot*, that thread becomes stronger and stronger. Ask the children to try to feel this thread of holy light as they perform *mitzvot*.

WHAT DO YOU HEAR?

When you listen to the still, small voice of your *neshamah*, you can gain much wisdom.
Put a check next to the questions your *neshamah* can help you answer.
Be prepared to discuss how your *neshamah* can help.

—What color socks should I wear?

—Is this a mean thing to say to someone?

—Should I do my homework?

—Should I help my friend?

—What time is it?

—What does 1+1 equal?

—How can I use my talents to the best of my ability?

—Am I being considerate?

WHAT CAN YOU DO?

Write the names of three people with whom you are close, such as friends or relatives.
Think about something special you would like to do for each person. It could be something to show the person how important she or he is to you. Or it could be something that would be helpful to the person. Next to each person's name, write what you would do.

Name	What I Can Do
_____	_____
_____	_____
_____	_____

86

AUTHOR! AUTHOR!

Jewish tradition teaches us that it is important to take care of our bodies *and* our souls. Imagine that you are an author writing a book called *A Jewish Guide to Health and Happiness*. Read the list of subjects below. Which four would you include in your chapters on keeping physically fit? Which four would you include in your chapters on caring for your soul?

- Exercise Is for Everyone
- The Importance of Being Lazy
- The Importance of Being Honest
- The Importance of Studying Torah
- The Joy of Junk Food
- Eating a Balanced Diet

- Saying "Thanks" by Saying *Brachot*
- Building a Dust Ball Collection
- Getting a Good Night's Rest
- Taking the Time to Do a *Mitzvah*
- Taking Time to Make a Mess
- Following Safety Rules

Write your answers on the lines below. Then list one additional subject you would include under each column.

Keeping Physically Fit   **Caring for Your Soul**

_____   _____

_____   _____

_____   _____

_____   _____

_____   _____

_____   _____

_____   _____

_____   _____

87

Teaching Goals

After studying this chapter, the student will understand:

1. When we observe Shabbat, we are creating an "island in time."

2. Observing Shabbat is a *mitzvah*. It is one of the Ten Commandments.

3. On Shabbat we rest and think. We celebrate God's creations as well as our own.

4. We keep Shabbat with special foods, prayers, candles, and song, and by spending time with friends and family. By our choice of activities on Friday evening and Saturday, we make the Sabbath holy.

Merry-go-rounds can be exciting and lots of fun. But what would it be like to ride one that never stopped? Do you think you might get dizzy or tired after a while? Would it become difficult to see the people around you as you went spinning by?

Working day after day can feel like being on a merry-go-round that doesn't stop. That is why we need a Day of Rest—a day to take satisfaction in all we have done and to enjoy the company of those we love. How might you spend such a day?

88

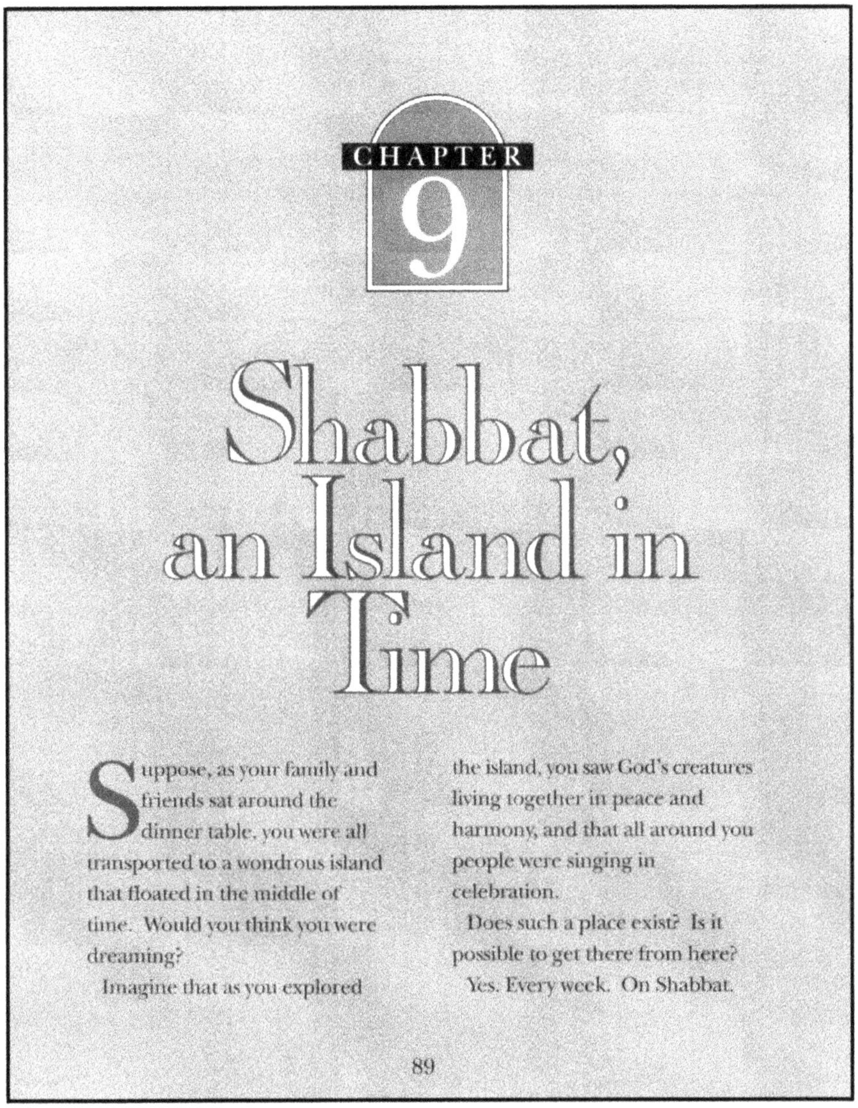

CHAPTER 9

Shabbat, an Island in Time

Suppose, as your family and friends sat around the dinner table, you were all transported to a wondrous island that floated in the middle of time. Would you think you were dreaming?

Imagine that as you explored the island, you saw God's creatures living together in peace and harmony, and that all around you people were singing in celebration.

Does such a place exist? Is it possible to get there from here?

Yes. Every week. On Shabbat.

89

Ask the students to share what they already know about Shabbat. List their responses on the chalkboard.

Ask students to write an acrostic using each letter in the word "Shabbat" to begin a sentence that describes this special day.

Take a Closer Look

Eli Wiesel, a Nobel Peace Prize winner, was invited to throw out the first ball of the 1986 World Series. He thanked the baseball commissioner but said he could not accept the honor because the game was on Shabbat, a holy day. The commissioner was so impressed by Wiesel's respect for the Sabbath that he invited him to throw the first ball of the second game, which was held on a weekday. Eli Wiesel was pleased and accepted.

A Note to the Teacher

By not engaging in weekday activities on Shabbat, Jews assert that material values alone do not create a rich life. By regularly bringing into our lives the joy of the sacred, we declare our freedom from the tyranny of physical reality.

Our sages teach us that Shabbat is like an *Island in Time* where peace and love refresh our souls, and where our bodies can relax in the warmth of the day.

Observing Shabbat Is a *Mitzvah*

On Shabbat, from sundown on Friday evening until the light of the first three stars on Saturday night, it is a *mitzvah* to leave the hustle and bustle of our daily lives. It is a *mitzvah* to join our families and community in honoring God the Creator.

> Shabbat reminds us of God's gift of freedom. Each week we remember that we were once slaves who worked without rest in the land of Egypt.

It is not always easy to stop working. Sometimes we are tempted to keep on going, to do just a little bit more and then a bit more after that. Before we know it, we may become slaves to our work or even to our play. Shabbat helps us let go of work and take time to rest and think.

Shabbat Is a Time of Celebration

Our lives are works of art, and on Shabbat we are like artists who stop creating and step back so that we can more clearly see and appreciate all we have done.

How do you feel when you have worked hard to complete something—a drawing, your homework, or cleaning your room? Are you often too tired to appreciate what a good job you've done? Are other family members sometimes too busy to share in your pride and pleasure?

Shabbat is the day of the week that has been set aside for celebrating God's creations as well as our own. It is the day when we are asked to put away our cares and unfinished work so that we can go off to the Island in Time.

90

From the Rabbi's Desk

Sometimes we think of Shabbat as less important than other holidays because it occurs frequently. But the Jewish principal is this: The frequent event takes precedence. Those who are closest to us and most present in our lives deserve our special attention. Too often we take them for granted. Shabbat is a regular visitor and, as such, merits a special place.

—DJW

This picture is part of a larger painting by Camille Pissarro. As the artist placed each dot with a brush, he could see only a small part of the painting. So, from time to time, he needed to stop and step back to make sure that all the dots came together to create a beautiful work of art.

In this same way, we need to step back from our daily lives so that we can more clearly see what we have done. Shabbat is the day we were given to do this. It is the day for us to remind ourselves of what makes our lives beautiful works of art.

Looking at this small part of Pissarro's painting, can you figure out what it is? Turn to page 94 to find out.

What the Torah Teaches

The Torah teaches us that God created the world on Days 1, 2, 3, 4, 5, and 6. But on the Seventh Day God stopped all work and rested. And God blessed the Seventh Day and made it holy.

It is said that on the Seventh Day Shabbat cried, "All the days of the week have partners. Day 1 has Day 2, Day 3 has Day 4, and Day 5 has Day 6. I am the only one who is alone!"

And God comforted Shabbat saying, "Do not fear. The Jewish people will be your partner."

Later, when God gave the Jewish people the Ten Commandments, we were told to "Remember the Sabbath day and keep it holy."

Shabbat is the only holiday included in the Ten Commandments. What does that tell you about Shabbat?

Take a Closer Look

The other days of the week are known in Hebrew simply as "first day," "second day," etc. Only the seventh day has a name—Shabbat.

A Note to the Teacher

Camille Pissarro
1830-1903

Camille Pissarro was born on the Caribbean island of St. Thomas. At the age of 11 he was sent to a boarding school near Paris, where he began to draw. Pissarro was a founding member of the Impressionist School of painting—the first great modern painter who was Jewish.

91

Activity Suggestion

Stage a Shabbat mini-dinner in the classroom with candles, grape juice, *hallah*, flowers, song, and stories. Recite the blessing.

Talk about the value of each ritual and what it adds to the Sabbath.

At another time, you might like to demonstrate the *Havdalah* ritual and discuss its meaning and purpose.

SHABBAT TRADITIONS

There are many ways to celebrate Shabbat and many traditions that have been passed on from generation-to-generation. Some people follow the traditions just as their parents taught them. Others create new traditions with their families and community.

Each Friday, before lighting the candles, it is a custom to give *tzedakah* to the needy. You can buy or make your own *tzedakah* box in which you put aside money for the poor.

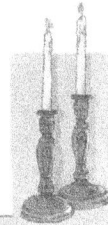

Shabbat begins with the lighting of candles and the blessing we recite over them. At least two candles are lit. Some people light one candle for each member of the family.

Before the meal we recite *Kiddush*. *Kiddush* means "holiness." The words of the *Kiddush* remind us that God made Shabbat a holy day. A *Kiddush* cup is filled with wine and held as the blessing is recited. Afterward, everyone takes a sip of the wine.

92

On Shabbat we eat a special bread called *hallah*. Two braided loaves of *hallah* are placed on the dinner table and covered with a cloth. Before we eat, we recite *Ha-Motzi*, the blessing over bread.

As Shabbat draws to a close, we perform the *Havdalah* ceremony. The Hebrew word *havdalah* means "separation." *Havdalah* creates an invisible line that separates Shabbat from the beginning of the new week. A braided candle, wine, and spices (such as cinnamon and cloves) are used in the ceremony. When we make *Havdalah*, we bring a pinch of Shabbat spice with us into the new week.

Shabbat is holy time— a time to join our friends and family in synagogue, where we pray and sing together, and study the lessons of Torah.

Jewish art often involves the creation of ritual objects, such as candlesticks, *Kiddush* cups, *hallah* covers, etc. These beautiful objects can help enhance our Shabbat experiences. Initiate an art project in your class to create one of these objects.

93

This might be an appropriate time to undertake an art project. Crayon Scratch is an interesting technique to try. Here's how it's done: Completely cover a piece of cardboard with patches of crayon color (do not use black), placing one color right next to another. Press hard to cover the board completely. Then brush black tempera paint over the entire surface to obscure the crayon. Let dry for several hours. Use a carpenter's nail to scratch a design through the black tempera surface revealing the underlying colors.

STEP BACK

You saw part of Camille Pissarro's painting on page 91. Here is the complete picture.

On Shabbat the natural order of the world is the same as it is Sunday through Friday. The sun rises and sets as it always does. Pine trees remain green and the sky blue. Birds continue to fly, snakes to crawl, and fish to swim. The difference on Shabbat is the difference in us—the Jewish people.

How will you make a difference on Shabbat? How can you help make Shabbat a holy day?

94

❖ ❖ ❖

Shabbat Spice

Long ago there lived a king who was very fond of eating. He liked his food cooked exactly right, with just enough spice and not too much salt.

Woe to the cook who served the king food he did not like, for the king would growl and roar like a hungry lion until the poor cook fainted from fright. But what honor and joy came to the cook who pleased the king, for no reward was too great for such a person.

One day the king was told of a rabbi who was an excellent cook. Excited by the news, the king sent word that he would like to dine with the rabbi. Pleased, the rabbi invited him for Shabbat dinner.

When the king arrived he was respectfully brought to the rabbi's table, which glowed from the light of the Shabbat candles.

First the king sipped the *Kiddush* wine. Then he took a bite of the crusty, warm *ḥallah*.

95

How to Teach the Story

Shabbat Spice

What's so special about a birthday cake? The difference between a birthday cake and an ordinary cake is not just the candles. It is really our attitude about it that makes it special.

In this story we will learn the secret of making ordinary food into special food—of working as partners with God to make an ordinary day into a holy one.

What kind of meal did the rabbi serve to the king?

Did the king enjoy the food?

What was the rabbi's secret spice?

Could the king buy such a spice? Why not?

Have you ever eaten a very simple meal and enjoyed it very much? Why was that?

Just as spices lend flavor to food, observing Shabbat is the Jewish way of imparting a special flavor to a period of time. Did the time (Friday evening) have anything to do with the way the food tasted? List things you think make up the "spice" called Shabbat.

What do you think makes the Shabbat meal special?

How can "Shabbat spice" make your life more enjoyable?

"My, my! What fragrant and delicious bread," he said, his nose twitching with delight.

As each course was served—the tangy vegetable soup, the chicken covered with honey glaze, and the rice piled high with toasted almonds and sweet raisins—the king smacked his lips and shook his head in amazement.

Before leaving, the king thanked the rabbi and said, "Each dish you served was like a taste of heaven. I beg you, please give me your recipes so that I might eat this well in my own home."

The rabbi smiled and gave the recipes to the king.

A week later, the king returned greatly upset. "Rabbi, my cook followed your recipes exactly as you gave them to me. Yet the food did not taste the same as it did in your house."

"Of course it didn't," said the rabbi. "It needed a pinch of Shabbat spice."

"Shabbat spice? You didn't tell me to add Shabbat spice. Where can I buy it?" asked the king.

"You cannot buy it," said the rabbi patiently.

The king roared, "I can buy anything I please. I am the king!"

"No one can *buy* Shabbat spice, for it is not for sale," explained the rabbi. "Shabbat spice is a *gift* and it is given freely to all who honor God by celebrating the Seventh Day. It is Shabbat that flavors food with a bit of heaven and offers us a taste of the World to Come."

❖   ❖   ❖

96

Making Shabbat a Holy Day

We can make Shabbat holy by resting from our weekday work and celebrating with those we love. We can honor God for the gift of Shabbat by lighting candles and saying *Kiddush* over Sabbath wine. We can bring *shalom bayit*, or peace into our homes, by not arguing with one another on Shabbat. And in synagogue, we can join other Jews in prayer and song and in the study of Torah.

If we do not welcome Shabbat with prayer and song, family and community, peace and delight, Shabbat will be like every other day of the week—like a wonderful island we do not visit.

Friday night and Saturday do not have the power to become Shabbat by themselves. They need us as partners with God to make them holy, to make them into Shabbat.

HEBREW LESSON

Shalom — שָׁלוֹם

Hello, Goodbye, or Peace

Shalom comes from the same root as the Hebrew word *shalem*, which means "whole" or "complete." Our tradition teaches us that as partners with God we must help bring peace into the world, for the world cannot be complete without it. When we greet each other by saying *shalom*, we are also wishing one another peace. And on Shabbat, when we say *"Shabbat Shalom,"* we are saying, "May you have a peaceful Shabbat."

97

Take a Closer Look

Help your students to understand that our partnership with God enables us to add the necessary "spice" that makes Shabbat so very different from the other days of the week. When we celebrate Shabbat, we add to its holiness through our attitudes and actions.

Teach the Hebrew Lesson

Have the students think of simple symbols that represent peace, such as a dove, a flower, people holding hands, etc. Have them draw the symbol using the Hebrew letters in the word *shalom* as part of their picture. The letters can be hidden in the drawing or used as part of the objects (*shin* made into flower, *lamed* into a tree, etc.).

Also see page 11 in this guide for Hebrew word games to practice the Hebrew vocabulary the students have learned.

WHAT KIND OF PERSON AM I?

Working hard at school and doing homework are important. But on Shabbat we are asked to leave these weekday activities behind.

On Shabbat we study Torah and the lessons of our sages so that we can feel closer to God and learn how to live as creatures made *b'tzelem Elohim*, in God's image.

Hillel taught us many important lessons. He said:

"If I am not for myself, who will be for me?
But if I am only for myself, what kind of person am I?
And if not now, when?"

In your own words, explain what Hillel meant and what he wanted to teach us.

_____

_____

_____

AN ISLAND IN TIME

On Shabbat we can refresh our souls by taking a break from our daily routines. We can light candles, go to synagogue, and sing *z'mirot*. We can also take time to enjoy God's creations by going for a walk in the park. These are just a few of the ways we can celebrate Shabbat and delight our souls.

What will you do to delight your soul on Shabbat?

_____

_____

_____

98

SH'LOM BAYIT

On Shabbat it is a special *mitzvah* to contribute to family peace and love, *sh'lom bayit*. During other days of the week, we may feel troubled or there may be quarrels in our family. On Shabbat, we make an extra effort to help keep *sh'lom bayit* by being considerate and thoughtful.

How could you help if:

1. Your family was seated at the dinner table and you saw that napkins had not been set out?

2. Your pet was hungry and it wasn't your turn to feed it but everyone else was busy?

3. Your mom or dad had a cold or was feeling tired?

IT'S ALL IN THE INGREDIENTS

Here's a jar of Shabbat spice. On the label, list four ingredients, such as lighting candles or singing *z'mirot*, that add "flavor" to Shabbat.

Shabbat Spice

99

After studying this chapter, the student will understand:

1. We pray for what we wish to become, not for what we want to be given.

2. The *siddur* contains prayers that ask for God's help, but more often our prayers offer thanks and praise to God.

3. It is important that we try to pray with sincerity, or from the heart. Doing this is known as praying with *kavannah*.

4. When we recite a blessing, we are thanking God. It is a way of showing our appreciation for all God's creations.

Have you ever felt that you could burst from the excitement of good news? Are there times when you are so happy you don't know whether to laugh or cry? And are there moments when you feel frightened or lonely, or angry with someone you love?

When these things happen, prayer can help us stop for a moment to get a clearer picture of what's really going on. Prayer can turn our feelings of excitement into words of thanks and appreciation for the goodness in our lives. Prayer can comfort us when we feel sad, frightened, or hurt. And prayer can remind us of God's love so that we can overcome feelings of loneliness, anger, or mistrust.

How can prayer help you sort out your feelings? How can it help you create a clearer picture of what you want or need to do?

100

CHAPTER 10

Speaking with God

Have you ever prayed to God asking for help? Did you tell someone else about your problem, or did you just talk with God?

Many people pray to God when they have problems. Prayer can help, but not always in the ways you might imagine.

How to Get Started

Ask your students if they ever talk to God. What subject or concerns do they talk about? How do they feel when they talk to God? How do they feel afterwards—stronger? Safer? Loved? Ask your students if they can think of another word for talking to God (*praying*).

From the Rabbi's Desk

When we teach our students about God, we must help them learn how to speak to God. Children have a natural instinct for prayer. At an early age, they learn the various sorts of prayers that we all share: praising God, thanking God, asking God for help. But there are many purposes to the prayers that we can teach our students.

Prayer does not always grant what we ask for, but it can teach us what we need. It helps us open ourselves up and assess our priorities. It establishes a relationship with others who pray and, most important, a relationship with God.

—DJW

Things to Talk About

Our sages taught that it is useless to pray to God to change what has already happened. For example, if for the third time in a week you lost another pair of gloves, it wouldn't help to pray to God for assistance in finding them. However, it could help to ask for the willingness to become more responsible for taking better care of them in the future.

Use the Photograph

Ask students to suggest another kind of photograph that might have been used in place of the dental office, and to describe what would be in the picture.

What We Pray For

Jewish tradition teaches us to pray for what we want to become—not for what we want to be given. Praying for a good grade on a test cannot help. But praying for the willingness to study hard can. Praying for a sports trophy cannot help. But praying for the patience to practice can. And praying for blue eyes when we have brown eyes, or for brown when we have blue, cannot help. But praying for the willingness to appreciate our God-given beauty and talents can.

Saying "Thank You" to God

There are prayers in our prayerbook, the *siddur*, that ask for God's help. But most Jewish prayers do not. Most of our prayers express gratitude for God's love and for the gifts of Creation. These prayers are a way of saying "thank you" to God.

Do you sometimes wonder why God needs our thanks? Do you wonder whether God would notice if we did not offer praise?

Our sages taught that prayers that ask God to change what has already happened are useless. For example, while sitting in a dentist's chair, it will not help to pray that you have no cavities. You either have cavities or you don't. However, it could help to pray for the willingness to become more responsible about caring for your teeth.

Name two ways you would like to become more responsible.

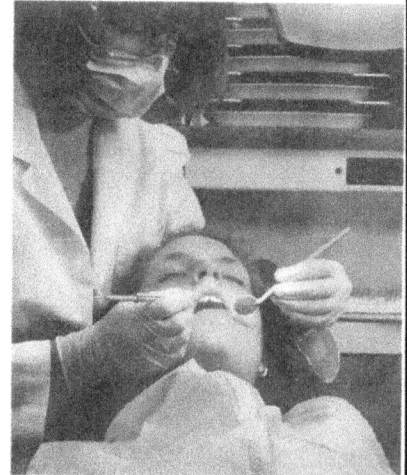

The truth is we pray to God more because *we* benefit from our prayers than because God needs them. Prayer, or *tefillah*, is not only a way of talking to God, it is also a way of reminding ourselves of what we need to do.

102

Activity Suggestion

Our sages say that not only people but all creation—the heavens and the earth, the sea and the sun—sings praises to God. Are there times when it feels as if the whole world and everything in it are singing? Can you remember one time in particular?

Ask students to imagine they are a particular animal and they can speak or write. Then have students tell or write what the animals might say to God. (Example: I am a giraffe. Thank you, God, for giving me such a long neck so that I can eat the tasty leaves at the tops of the trees and for making trees so that I have leaves to eat.)

What Makes Prayer Work?

Prayers of thanks always "work." When we thank God for the goodness in our lives, we feel complete because we have shown respect and appreciation.

When we pray, it is important to concentrate on the words we say. It is important to say each word from the heart—with feeling. This is called *kavannah*.

We say, "Open my mouth, God, and my lips will declare Your praise." This reminds us that God is the source of all our abilities, even our ability to praise God.

Sometimes we pray sitting down, at other times we stand. Sometimes we pray in song, at other times in silence. And sometimes we pray alone, while at other times we are with family and friends in the synagogue.

When we are alone, we often think only of ourselves. If we always prayed *by ourselves*, we might become selfish and pray only *for ourselves*. Praying together is the first step in the Jewish path toward working together. And working together is the first step toward making our world a better place for all God's creations.

103

Kavannah

Discuss with the class what it means to "go through the motions" of an act. Is it possible to do something that is meant to be kind but to do it in an unkind way? To do something that is meant to be good but to do it in a bad way? Ask the class to suggest illustrations of this point. For example, suppose you are feeling tired and irritable, but you offer to help a friend who is having difficulty in math and then you speak impatiently to him or her. Do you think it is useful or fair to offer your help when you are feeling resentful and unwilling to change your mood? Would it be better to work on your attitude or choose another time to help your friend?

Discuss the meaning of *kavannah* with the class. How does it relate to going to religious school? Is it possible to learn if you are not really trying? What about prayer? Are you really praying if you just say the words without feeling anything? Ask the students to suggest other areas of life where *kavannah* is important.

Use the Photograph

The minimum Jewish community required for public prayer is called a *minyan*. A *minyan* is made up of at least ten people who have reached the age of *bar* or *bat mitzvah*.

Blessings can remind us of the many "everyday wonders" in our lives, such as the taste of strawberries and the shape of snowflakes.

Ask the students to draw a picture of or write about a favorite everyday wonder. Then ask them to compose a blessing that expresses appreciation for this wonder.

Activity Suggestion

Have each child make a book of blessings. The students can write a blessing on each page (including those in this book and others as well), and then they can illustrate them.

Or, you might create a "big book" of blessings with one page made by each student, or a large blessing poster to display in the classroom.

WHAT A BLESSING!

The Jewish people believe that all life is extraordinary and that God is the source of its wonder. When we see, taste, hear, or smell one of life's delights, we express our appreciation by reciting a blessing.

FOR THE FIRST TIME
Jews celebrate the excitement of doing something for the first time by reciting a blessing called the *Shehecheyanu*. When you do something new, celebrate by saying:

בָּרוּךְ אַתָּה יְיָ אֱלֹהֵינוּ מֶלֶךְ הָעוֹלָם,
שֶׁהֶחֱיָנוּ וְקִיְּמָנוּ וְהִגִּיעָנוּ לַזְּמַן הַזֶּה.

Blessed are You, Adonai our God, Ruler of the universe, who has given us life, sustained us, and brought us to this day.

THE WONDERS OF CREATION
Saying a blessing as you enjoy a sunrise, a majestic mountain, or a shooting star thanks God for the wonders of creation:

בָּרוּךְ אַתָּה יְיָ אֱלֹהֵינוּ מֶלֶךְ הָעוֹלָם,
עֹשֶׂה מַעֲשֵׂה בְרֵאשִׁית.

Blessed are You, Adonai our God, Ruler of the universe, the Source of Creation.

104

FRAGRANT FLOWERS

In the spring, when you stroll through a park or a garden, does your nose tingle with delight as you inhale the fragrance of flowers in bloom? Our ancestors enjoyed these same scents, and you can repeat their ancient words:

בָּרוּךְ אַתָּה יְיָ אֱלֹהֵינוּ מֶלֶךְ הָעוֹלָם,
בּוֹרֵא עִשְׂבֵי בְשָׂמִים.

Blessed are You, Adonai our God, Ruler of the universe, who creates fragrant plants.

A RAINBOW

Sometimes, after a storm has passed and the sun comes out, you can see a rainbow arching across the sky. When you do, you can say:

בָּרוּךְ אַתָּה יְיָ אֱלֹהֵינוּ מֶלֶךְ הָעוֹלָם,
זוֹכֵר הַבְּרִית וְנֶאֱמָן בִּבְרִיתוֹ
וְקַיָּם בְּמַאֲמָרוֹ.

Blessed are You, Adonai our God, Ruler of the universe, who remembers the Covenant, is faithful to it, and keeps Your promise.

A STORM

Have you ever been startled by a great clap of thunder or buckets of rain pouring down in a storm? The next time you are, you can recite these words:

בָּרוּךְ אַתָּה יְיָ אֱלֹהֵינוּ מֶלֶךְ הָעוֹלָם,
שֶׁכֹּחוֹ וּגְבוּרָתוֹ מָלֵא עוֹלָם.

Blessed are You, Adonai our God, Ruler of the universe, whose power and might fill the world.

Take a Closer Look

Brainstorm a list of blessings that we recite in our daily lives. Ask each student to choose one and to recite it during the coming week whenever appropriate. Encourage the students to report back at the next session. How did it feel? Was it hard to remember to do it? Did it make that event feel more important? etc.

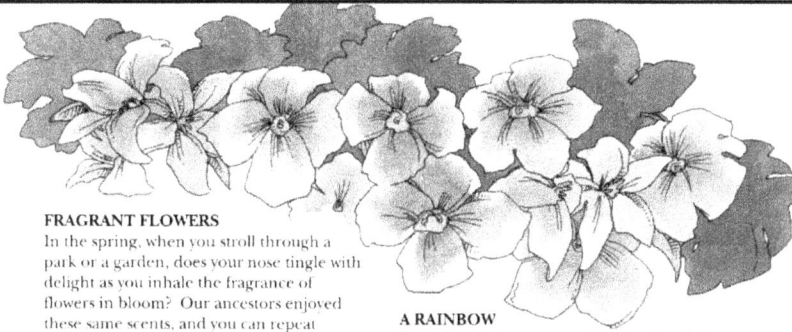

Select a short prayer and recite it together as a group. Then ask the students to recite the same prayer to themselves. Is that experience different? Which do they prefer? Why?

Ask the students to put a particular traditional prayer into their own words. Ask how it feels to recite a prayer that has been said by generations and generations of our people around the world. How does it feel to say it in their own words?

Praying Together

By praying with others, we are reminded that we are not alone—we are part of a much larger "family." And by participating in synagogue services we become partners in prayer with the entire community, connected to one another and to God.

In fact, most Jewish prayers are intended to be said when we pray together as a group. That is why we say, "Blessed be You, *our* God," not "*my* God." That is why we say, "Help *us* lie down in peace," not "Help *me* lie down in peace."

Even when we pray by ourselves, we say the same words that we recite with our congregation. We do this because we believe that a Jew in prayer is never alone. When we pray, we are united with Jews throughout the world and throughout all time.

By praying as a community, we let God know that not only do we care about ourselves but also about God's other creations. By praising God, we are reminded of God's goodness and love for us. And when we are filled with that love and say thank you from deep within our souls, we are strengthened.

In every country and every age in which Jews have lived, Shabbat prayers have been recited on Friday night.

Jews in Argentina, Israel, France, and Greece all sit down to read the *Haggadah* on the 15th of *Nisan*, the first night of Passover.

And when you light the Hanukkah candles and chant the *brachah*, you are doing as Jews did in the time of Columbus and as they do today, even in places as far away as South Africa and Brazil.

106

HEBREW LESSON

Tefillah— תְּפִלָה
"Prayer"

Tefillah means "prayer" in Hebrew. It comes from the same root as the Hebrew word that means "to judge." Our tradition teaches us that when we pray, we judge ourselves. Prayer helps us see how we are living as creatures made *b'tzelem Elohim* and how we can improve. When we pray, we praise God for the good in our lives and ask for the willingness to become better people.

SHEHECHEYANU

The *Shehecheyanu* blessing is recited on Jewish holidays and in celebration of first-time events. For example, you can say *Shehecheyanu* the first time you eat a fruit in its season, or learn a new skill, or even when you wear a pair of sneakers for the first time.

List five first-time events you can make more special by reciting the *Shehecheyanu*.

_____

_____

_____

_____

_____

_____

_____

_____

_____

_____

_____

_____

_____

107

Teach the Hebrew Lesson

While this lesson concerns the world *tefillah*, there are several other Hebrew words presented in the chapter: *siddur*, *kavannah*, and *minyan*. You can actively use these words in English sentences in the classroom. For example, "Michael, please pass out the *siddurim*." The more you do this, the more familiar your students will become with the Hebrew vocabulary.

Students can "act out" the Hebrew words they have accumulated while others guess which word they chose. A variation of this game is to draw a clue picture for words on the chalkboard and ask students to say the Hebrew word for the picture.

WHAT WORKS BEST FOR YOU?

What helps you pray with *kavannah*? Underline what works best for you.

1 I feel best praying
  a. by myself
  b. with my family
  c. with kids my own age
  d. with my congregation

2 I feel best praying
  a. in synagogue
  b. in my room
  c. outdoors
  d. in religious school

3 I feel best praying
  a. silently
  b. aloud
  c. with music
  d. in Hebrew

4 I feel best praying
  a. words of thanks to God
  b. for the willingness to help myself
  c. for the willingness to help others
  d. for things I want

WHAT BELONGS IN A *SIDDUR*?

The Jewish prayerbook is called a *siddur.* Just as the lines on a tennis court help us know when a ball falls out of bounds, the *siddur* helps us know what kind of prayer is appropriate and what kind is out of bounds.

Check the prayers you think belong in a prayerbook. Be prepared to discuss why you think they belong in the *siddur*.

108

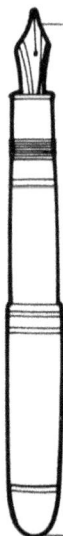

From the Rabbi's Desk

Children often ask why we have a prayerbook—why they cannot simply pray what is in their hearts. The answer is that of course they can, but there are other elements involved in a prayerbook. Not only does it connect us to a community, but it also reminds us of what really matters. When we look in the prayerbook, we find the desires of human beings, refined over centuries to distill what is truly important and worthy in them.

—DJW

STEP BY STEP

Praying for the willingness to try your best can help you feel more confident and determined. But praying is only one rung on the "Ladder of Achievement."

Here is a list of steps you can take to do well on a test. Place each step in its proper order on the ladder.

- **Read and follow the test directions.**
- **Study for the test.**
- **Pray for the willingness to study.**
- **Do your homework.**
- **Pay attention in class.**

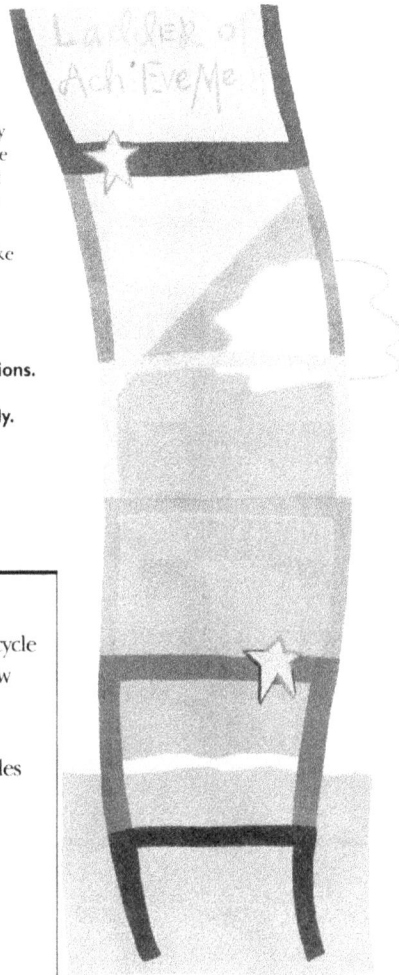

___ Prayer to be given a new bicycle

___ Blessing recited on riding a new bicycle

___ Blessing recited on seeing a rainbow

___ Prayer for someone who is ill

___ Prayer for money to grow on trees

___ Blessing recited over Shabbat candles

___ Prayer for peace in the world

___ Blessing recited over spilt milk

___ Blessing recited over bread

___ Prayer that a lost toy will be found

109

After studying this chapter, the student will understand:

1. When we make mistakes and feel we have distanced ourselves from God, we can do *teshuvah*, correct the mistake and return to God.

2. *Teshuvah* involves taking responsibility for one's actions.

3. When we change our behavior, our request for forgiveness is granted.

4. When we forgive others for their mistakes, God forgives us for ours.

5. On Yom Kippur, Jews gather together as a community to ask for God's forgiveness.

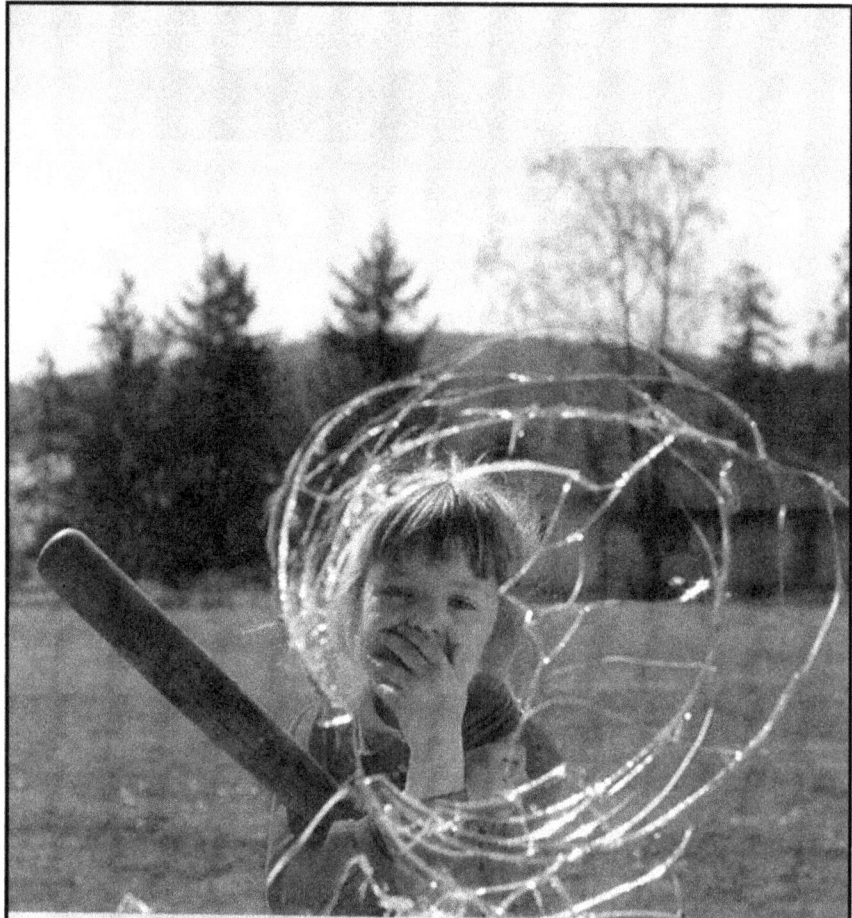

Like parents who forgive, God forgives our mistakes and gives us the chance to do better. This girl hit a baseball into her neighbor's window. She didn't do it on purpose, but the glass shattered. What should she do now? What can she do in the future to avoid this kind of accident? How does correcting our mistakes help us grow?

110

CHAPTER 11

God's Forgiveness

Did you ever do something you hoped no one would find out about? Maybe you were careless and broke something that wasn't yours. Or maybe you said something unkind to your brother or sister, or to a friend. Did you feel bad and want to hide the evidence or run away? When you thought about apologizing for what you did or said, did you wish someone would meet you halfway to make it easier?

The story is told of a princess who strayed far from the royal palace. She wanted to return home, but she knew the journey back would take 100 days. The princess felt too tired and weak to

111

From the Rabbi's Desk

If we are to teach our students that sin is real, we cannot stop with that teaching alone. All people sin, for no one is perfect. Therefore we must also teach that forgiveness and repentance are real. Repenting is a way to return to the original relationship of closeness to God and to the person we have hurt. True repentance is the "answer" to the question of what we can do to renew and revive ourselves. *Teshuvah* means that there is always hope.

—DJW

Take a Closer Look

Write the word "atone" on the chalkboard. It is said that to "atone" for our sins is to ask for forgiveness and do our best to be better people.

What two words do your students see in the word "atone"? When we do *teshuvah* we are *at one* with God.

Use the Photograph

Why did the girl in the picture tell her coach what she had done wrong? Could she have kept it a secret? Why did she choose not to do so?

Ask students to consider this situation:
Suppose your closest friend had hurt you, either with an unkind word or by getting you into trouble at school.

What attitude would you take toward your friend? Why?

What would this friend's responsibility be to you? Is it enough just to be sorry when you harmed another person? Why or why not?

make the trip, and so she wept. Then her mother, the queen, sent her a message saying, "My daughter, return as far as you can and I will travel the remaining distance to meet you."

The rabbis explain that in this same way, God says to us, "Return to Me and I will return to you."

Returning to God

To return to God means to return to God's ways—to do *teshuvah.*

If you hurt another person, the first step of *teshuvah* is to apologize to that person and try to correct your mistake. The next step is to turn toward God and ask for forgiveness. And the final step of *teshuvah*, returning to God, is to change your behavior—to try harder to live as a creature made in God's image.

We All Make Mistakes

In the Torah, the book of Genesis tells how our ancestors Adam and Eve ate the forbidden fruit in the Garden of Eden. When God asked Adam if he had eaten the fruit, Adam blamed Eve. When God spoke with Eve, she blamed the snake. Neither Adam nor Eve took responsibility for their actions.

To this day, many of us have the same difficulty. It takes courage to admit we have made a mistake. However, it is comforting to know that when we do take responsibility and return to God, God welcomes us.

This girl loves playing soccer and wanted to win the game more than anything. Unfortunately, she cheated by kicking someone on the other team. She hoped the referee wouldn't notice. He didn't. But after the game the girl told her coach what she had done. What do you think the coach is saying to her? What would you say?

112

Add the word *teshuvah* to your display of Hebrew words. Include this new vocabulary word in the suggested activities on page 11 in this guide.

How to Teach the Story

The Thief's Secret

Explain to the students that the story they will read is about a girl who steals something, and a very strict nobleman who was very harsh and unforgiving.

What did Elana steal? Why?

Do you think the nobleman's punishment was fair? Why or why not?

What was Elana's secret? Did you believe her? (How long does it usually take for a seed to grow into a fruit-bearing tree?)

Why wouldn't Elana plant the seed? The nobleman's friend? The nobleman's wife? The nobleman?

HEBREW LESSON

Teshuvah — תְּשׁוּבָה
"Return" or "Repentance"

We do *teshuvah* by repenting for our mistakes, taking responsibility for our actions, and apologizing to those we have hurt. When we change our behavior, our request for forgiveness is answered by God.

When we are sincere, God always answers by taking us back. Sometimes the answer comes through the still, small voice of our souls and sometimes through the forgiving voice of a person we have wronged.

When we are unkind or dishonest, or ignore opportunities to do good, we lose a chance to be the best we can be. Each chance we are given is precious. Each opportunity we ignore is our loss. Fortunately, God is forgiving and provides us with many chances.

As difficult as it may be to admit our own mistakes, it sometimes can be more difficult to forgive others for theirs, even if they apologize. Feelings of anger or hurt can get in the way of our remembering that none of us is perfect.

It is helpful to remember that just as we are worthy of forgiveness, so are other people. Our sages teach us that when we forgive others for their mistakes, God forgives us for ours.

❖　　❖　　❖

The Thief's Secret

Once there was a rich and powerful nobleman who had a terrible temper. He could be very harsh and unforgiving.

One day a poor servant girl named Elana was cleaning the pantry. Seeing no one around, she quickly put three plums in her apron pocket to bring to her younger brothers who were very hungry. But a guard saw her and reported the theft.

113

Moments later, Elana was brought before the angry nobleman who shouted, "Take her to the dungeon and keep her chained to the wall until she is old and gray!"

The nobleman's friends and family gasped at the harshness of his judgment.

But Elana remained calm and said, "My lord, I accept your judgment, though it is a pity my mother's secret will be locked up with me."

"Your mother's secret?" asked the nobleman. "What might that be?"

Elana replied, "My mother knew how to plant pomegranate seeds so that they bore fruit the very next day."

"Hmm," thought the nobleman to himself. "If overnight I could grow fields of this delicious fruit, I would become the richest man in all the land."

So he said to Elana, "If your words are true, show me how it is done."

The nobleman and his family and friends followed Elana into

114

Take a Closer Look

Ask the class to consider what you can do if you feel a person in authority (teacher, parent) has given you an unfair punishment. Are you always the best judge of whether a punishment is fair or unfair?

the garden. With great curiosity they watched her dig a deep hole.

When the hole was ready, Elana said, "The seed will bear fruit overnight only if it is planted by someone who has never taken property that belonged to someone else. Since I am a thief, I cannot plant it. Who among you can?"

The nobleman turned to his closest friend and said, "You may have the honor."

Sheepishly, his friend said, "I'm afraid I cannot, for when I was a young man I took my father's watch."

"Then you, dear wife, please honor us by planting the seed," the nobleman said, extending his hand to her.

"My beloved husband," she replied, "I too have been guilty of taking something that was not mine. In a moment of jealousy, I took my sister's locket when we were girls."

One by one the nobleman asked all who were present to plant the seed. And one by one they told the story of how they had taken something that did not belong to them.

"My lord, may I suggest that the honor go to you," said Elana, handing him the seed. But the seed dropped through his fingers as he remembered picking fresh herbs without permission from his neighbor's garden .

Shaking his head, the nobleman said, "You are a clever girl. You have taught me that none of us is perfect. I grant you pardon for your misdeed and invite you to take as much food as you need to feed your family."

From that day on, before judging others the nobleman always reminded himself of his own misdeeds.

———

The people in this story each took something that did not belong to them. Do you think it is all right to do something you know is wrong just because other people do it? Why or why not?

———

Activity Suggestion

Hold a mock trial of Elana, with a defense lawyer, prosecutor, judge, jury, and witnesses.

? Things to Talk About

What lesson did the nobleman learn in the story?

Do you think in the future he will excuse all thieves? Do you think excusing all thieves would be a good idea? Explain.

If you were the judge, what kind of punishment, if any, would you have given Elana? (It should be emphasized that the lesson learned was not that wrongdoing should go unpunished, but that judgment should be tempered with compassion for the human imperfection we all share.)

Take a Closer Look

In the story it seems that just about everybody had taken something that didn't belong to him or her.

Do you think this is true in real life?

What are some examples of what people can take that probably won't result in their being jailed (items taken from family members or supplies from school or work)?

Since people know it is wrong to steal, why do you think so many people steal, or are tempted to?

Does the fact that so many people take things mean that stealing is not wrong?

Things to Talk About

We all make mistakes. In Hebrew we sometimes refer to a mistake as a *het*, or sin. In Hebrew, however, the word carries a different meaning than in English. Committing a *het* is more like missing the mark. It is as though we aim for perfect behavior but sometimes miss. Ask your students if they have ever intended to act correctly but somehow missed the mark. Have the students share examples and discuss them.

When we do *teshuvah*, we must ask the person we have wronged to forgive us. Sometimes we must ask God to forgive us. What are some sins that require us to ask the forgiveness of another person? What are some sins that require us to ask forgiveness from God?

Sometimes we are asked to forgive others for wrongs they have done to us. Have you ever done this? Is it easy to do? Why or why not? Why is it important to forgive others?

Thinking Is Not Doing

Just as *thinking* about a *mitzvah* is not the same as *doing* it, having a mean thought or angry feeling is not the same as doing something mean or hurtful.

Sometimes when we are upset with other people, we may have unkind thoughts or feelings. When we do, it is important to remember that such thoughts or feelings are hurtful only to us, not to the other person. In fact, we need not apologize to anyone for our thoughts. Instead, we turn to God so we can be comforted by God's love.

A Special Day for Repentance

As individuals, we can do *teshuvah* on any day of the year. But on Yom Kippur, the Day of Atonement, Jews come together as a community to ask for God's forgiveness.

On Rosh Hashanah we begin preparing ourselves for the Day of Atonement. We think about what we have done during the past year and how we can do better in the coming year. During the next week and a half, the Ten Days of Repentance, we ask forgiveness from people we have hurt and we try to correct the wrong acts we have done.

Just as we are partners with God, so we are also partners with one another. That is why when we ask to be forgiven for our own sins, we also pray that other people will be forgiven for theirs. That is why we say, "Please forgive *us*," not "Please forgive *me*."

God Welcomes Us Back

God welcomes us back every day of the year, not just on Yom Kippur. And because God is merciful, God takes us back with love.

The Gates of Return are always open, and all who enter by doing *teshuvah* are greeted with love. Every day is filled with opportunities to start fresh—to live a better life, to live as a partner with God.

116

A Note to the Teacher

Jewish tradition teaches that God judges people on Rosh Hashanah but does not seal the decree until Yom Kippur. The period between Rosh Hashanah and Yom Kippur, known as the Ten Days of Repentance, provides an opportunity for self-examination, repentance, and renewed resolution to live an ethical life.

WE ALL MAKE MISTAKES

Since we all are human, we all make mistakes. But we are not always willing to do *teshuvah*. Why is it sometimes difficult to do *teshuvah*?

_____

_____

What would make it easier for you to do *teshuvah*?

_____

_____

It can be tempting to blame someone else for the mistakes you make, but in your heart you always know the truth. How can you grow by taking responsibility for the mistakes you make? How can you gain the respect and trust of others when you do?

REMEMBER

The three steps of *teshuvah* are:

1 TURN Apologize **2** GOD CHANGE YOUR BEHAVIOR

RETURNING ONE STEP AT A TIME

Sometimes, after we have argued with someone we love, the worst part can be the separation—not seeing or speaking to the person. We may feel more lonely than angry. We may feel more ashamed of our behavior and less certain of how wrong the other person's behavior was.

What three steps can you take to make things better?

Step 1: _____

Step 2: _____

Step 3: _____

117

Teaching Goals

After studying this chapter, the student will understand:

1. Faith in God gives us the courage and willingness to speak up for what is right. Faith keeps us strong.

2. Many questions about God remain unanswered. It is sometimes difficult to have faith.

3. The words of Torah keep us close to God. They comfort us and give us hope.

4. We show our faith and trust in God through our actions.

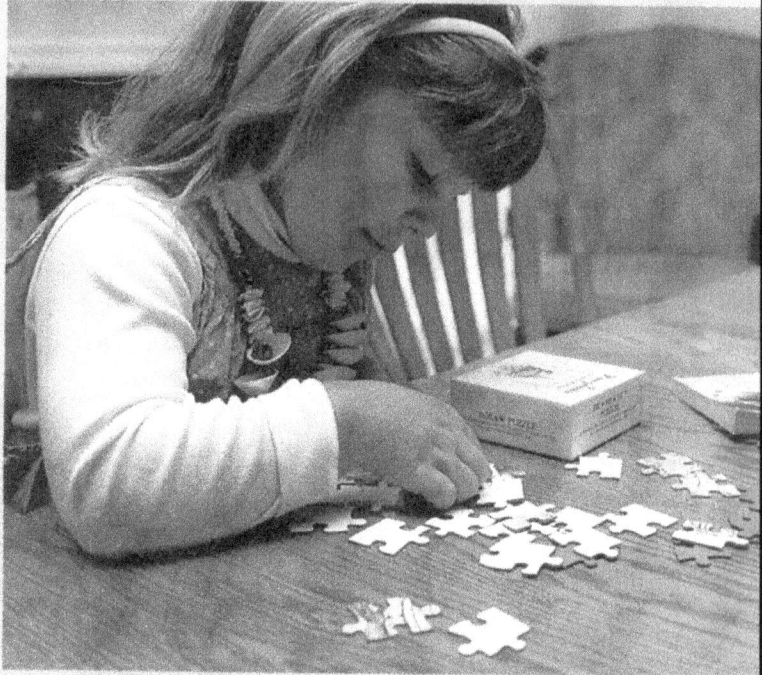

It's fun to put the pieces of a jigsaw puzzle together so you can see the whole picture. But suppose you were given only 25 of the 1,000 pieces of the puzzle. How many of those pieces do you think might fit together? How much of the picture would you be able to see?

Understanding God is like trying to imagine what a completed puzzle looks like when you only have a few of the pieces. Because we are human, we can never understand God completely—we can never see the entire picture. But as we grow older, and learn from others and from our own experience, we find more of the missing pieces and we can understand more.

What have you learned about God since you began reading this book? What questions do you still have?

118

CHAPTER 12

Faith Makes Us Strong

Can you remember a time when you felt unhappy or upset? Perhaps you didn't get the part you wanted in a school play, or perhaps a relative became very sick. Maybe you weren't invited to a classmate's party, or maybe you couldn't play a favorite sport because you were injured. Did you wonder when God would make things better, or even *if* God *could* make things better?

119

How to Get Started

Bring a jigsaw puzzle to class (make sure it's a simple one with 10-25 pieces). As the students arrive, give each one a puzzle piece and invite the whole class to put the puzzle together.

Explain to students that while it's fun to put the pieces of a jigsaw puzzle together one-by-one until you can see the whole picture, understanding God is like trying to imagine what a thousand-piece puzzle looks like when you have only a few of the pieces.

This is an appropriate time to begin a discussion of what your students have learned about God and what questions they still have.

From the Rabbi's Desk

Nothing could be more important than the feeling that someone always cares and truly understands. A child who believes in God's concern is a child who trusts in the goodness of the world. Such trust is a priceless legacy to a child. And in teaching children trust, we become more trusted, and perhaps more trusting, our-selves, for the special perspective of children can help foster our own faith. Our students can remind us that it is important not only to attempt to understand the world, but to cherish it as well.

—DJW

How to Teach the Story

The Daughters of Zelophechad

After reading the story, ask your students:

How do you think the daughters of Zelophechad felt before they spoke up?

Why do you think they spoke up?

Is it important to speak up for what you think is right?

Has there ever been a time when you felt the need to speak up about something that was important to you? How did it feel? Was it easy or difficult to do? How can God help in those situations? How does God want you to behave?

❖   ❖   ❖

The Daughters of Zelophechad

The Torah tells the story of five sisters who had great faith and trust in God.

Before the Children of Israel entered the Promised Land, God told Moses to count the number of men in the community and then divide the land among them.

When the five daughters of Zelophechad—Machlah, Noah, Chaglah, Milcah, and Tirtzah—heard that the land would be given to men but not to women, they knew they must speak up. Their father had died and there was no man in their household.

"God is just and merciful to all," they said. "God will not allow the portion of land that is due our family to be given to another."

And so the five sisters stepped forward and spoke to Moses and the elders of the community saying, "We have neither father nor brother. However, it is only fair that we receive our portion of the Land."

Impressed by what they said, Moses repeated their words to God. And God said, "The daughters of Zelophechad are right. They must be given their fair portion. Let it

120

From the Rabbi's Desk

Another word for faith is *bitachon*, which means "trust." To have faith is to trust in the ultimate goodness of the world. To help children have *bitachon* is to fortify their souls against the trials of life.

—DJW

become law that the rights of all daughters be protected."

Like Abraham and Moses, the five sisters—Machlah, Noah, Chaglah, Milcah, and Tirtzah—had deep faith in God's fairness and justice. Their faith in God gave them the courage and willingness to speak up for what they believed was right.

❖   ❖   ❖

Having Faith Can Be Difficult

Judaism teaches us to have faith in God—*emunah*. But having faith is not always easy. In fact, it can be especially difficult when you don't feel good about what has happened to you or to those you love. You may ask many questions: Why did God let this

happen? Didn't God hear my prayers? Doesn't God care when people suffer?

HEBREW LESSON

Emunah —

אֱמוּנָה

Faith, Trust, or Belief

Emunah means faith or belief in God. It is also the word that describes God's faithfulness and trust in us. As Jews, we believe and trust in God and in God's faithfulness to us.

121

A cinquain is a form of poetry in which five lines are used in the following way:

1 noun
2 adjectives
3 verbs ending in "ing"
4 adjectives
1 noun (a synonym for the noun used in the first line)

Ask each student to write a cinquain describing God or one of God's creations.

Here is an example:

Creator
Merciful, just
Giving, loving, understanding
Forgiving, kind, good, powerful
God

Take a Closer look

Ask students to imagine that they live in a deep small hole. When they look up, all they can see is a little bit of the sky. Might they think that is all there is because that is all they can see? Perhaps this is how we feel living in God's world and not knowing all there is to know.

Teach the Hebrew Lesson

The word *emunah* is often used as a girl's Hebrew name. What might a parent wish for the child by naming her *Emunah*?

The word *amen* comes from the same root as *emunah*. When we hear a prayer and say "amen," we are saying that we agree with what was just said. It is like saying, "I believe that!"

This would be a good time to review all the Hebrew words the students have learned in the book. See the suggested review activities on page 11 in this guide.

Hang a large world map on the bulletin board. Give each student a large Band-Aid. On the Band-Aids, ask students to write (with a black marker) something they can do to make the world a better place. Each student can then remove the paper on the back of the Band-Aid and tape it to the map.

We believe that God does not want people to suffer and that God gives us the strength to help ourselves and others.

Years ago many children became very sick from a virus called polio. Some of them were paralyzed by the disease; they couldn't run or walk or play. Scientists worked day and night to discover a way to prevent the awful illness. And they finally succeeded! The polio vaccine you received will help keep you healthy and well.

Throughout the ages, people have asked these same questions. Sometimes they realized that people, not God, caused the suffering. And sometimes they understood that God's way of answering our prayers is by giving us the willingness and strength to help ourselves and others in need.

Even our greatest rabbis and teachers haven't known the answers to all our questions about God. Some questions remain unanswered.

For example, while we may know the scientific reasons why fires, floods, earthquakes, illness, and airplane accidents occur, we may never understand why the pain and suffering they cause can happen in God's world. When such tragedies occur, we may question where God is or even if there is a God.

122

A Love Letter

There once was a great king who married a very wise young woman. But the day after their wedding celebration, the king set out on a long journey.

Days, weeks, and months passed but the king did not return. One, two, and three years passed and still there was no sign of him.

The young woman's friends told her to forget her husband and find someone new to love. But she read and reread a letter the king had given her.

The letter said, "Dearest wife, I will always love you and be faithful to you. I only ask that you put your trust in me."

When she read these words, the wise young woman was comforted and cheered, and her love and faith in her husband grew stronger.

Many years later the king returned and his wife joyfully greeted him. With tears in his eyes the king said, "My beloved, ours is truly a marriage of love and trust."

And so it has been with the Jewish people. Even when God seemed far away, our people kept their faith. And in every generation, the words of Torah have been like a love letter from God, comforting us and giving us hope.

❖ ❖ ❖

Take a Closer Look

The national anthem of the State of Israel is *Hatikvah*, "The Hope." It was written over 100 years ago, before the state was born, when a Jewish homeland was still only a dream.

The words are: "As long as a Jewish heart beats, and as long as Jewish eyes look toward the east, then our 2,000-year hope, to be a free nation in the land of Zion and Jerusalem, is not lost."

In a cellar where Jews hid from the Nazis during World War II, the following words were written on the wall: "I believe in the sun even when it is not shining. I believe in love even when I do not feel it. And I believe in God even when God is silent."

Ask:

What do you think the writer meant? Are there times when you feel God is "silent"? What can you do to remind yourself of God's constant presence in the world? What can you do to remind others of God's presence?

Emunah **Makes Us Strong**

Emunah helps us remain faithful partners of God even when we are filled with questions and doubts.

Emunah can strengthen us when we are having difficulty believing in ourselves. This does not mean that we will always get what we want. It does mean that when we have faith, God gives us the courage and strength to do the best we can with what we have. Faith and trust in God also give us hope that tomorrow will be better.

Sometimes after people experience a personal tragedy, such as the accidental death of a friend or relative, they work to keep others from suffering in the same way.

For example, one mother whose daughter was killed in a car accident caused by a drunk driver founded an organization called Mothers Against Drunk Driving (MADD). Although she felt very angry, instead of doing something hurtful, she worked to prevent terrible accidents from happening to other children.

As Jews, we show our faith and trust in God through our actions. Our *emunah* helps us see hope and the opportunity for good even in difficult situations. This may mean visiting a friend or relative who is ill or sad. Or, discovering the importance of letting people know we love them. Or, it can mean developing patience and working hard to make tomorrow better.

Our sages teach us that God performs miracles for us, though we often are unaware of them. They are the miracles of the rising sun, human creativity, and our ability to grow, learn, and help others. The more we have faith and are able to reach out to God—in good times and in bad—the more we are able to see the miracles and become part of them.

124

The miracle of human creativity is a constant reminder of God's presence in our lives. We express our gratitude by thanking God and by working with others to make a better world—bringing our acts of loving kindness to God's Creation. How can you thank God for the miracles in your life? How can you work with others to make a better world?

125

Things to Talk About

Now is a good time to ask your students to evaluate the book they have studied. Have them discuss what they have learned.

What new ideas did they gain?

Did the stories they read help them understand the lessons? Which story was their favorite?

In what ways did the class discussions stimulate their thinking?

What did the activities teach them about themselves?

In what ways did they grow during the year?

Ask each student to prepare a brief paragraph, poem, or artwork that depicts something meaningful they learned during the year. Publish them all in a class book and distribute copies as a remembrance of the experience.

MAKING YOUR DREAMS COME TRUE

Our faith in God can strengthen us by giving us hope in the future. We show our faith by living as partners with God.

1 Name one hope or dream you have for yourself.

_____

What can you do as a partner with God to help make that dream come true?

_____

2 Name one hope or dream you have for your family.

_____

What can you do as a partner with God to help make that dream come true?

_____

3 Name one hope or dream you have for the Jewish people.

_____

What can you do as a partner with God to help make that dream come true?

_____

4 Name one hope or dream you have for everyone in the world.

_____

What can you do as a partner with God to help make that dream come true?

_____

126

PIECES OF A PUZZLE

You have come to the end of this book but not to the end of your learning. Fill in the pieces of the puzzle below by writing four things you learned about God and our partnership with God.

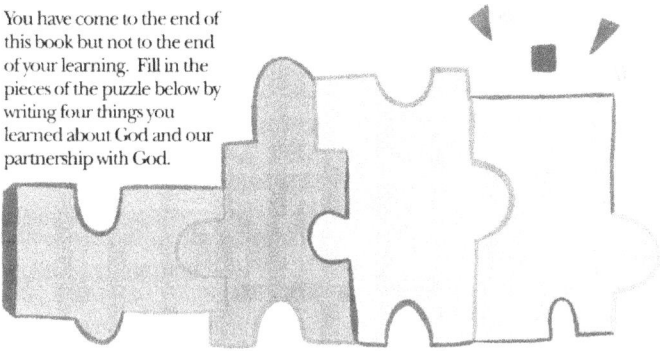

Because we cannot know everything about God, you probably still have questions you would like answered. Write four questions on the pieces of the puzzle that do not yet fit together for you.

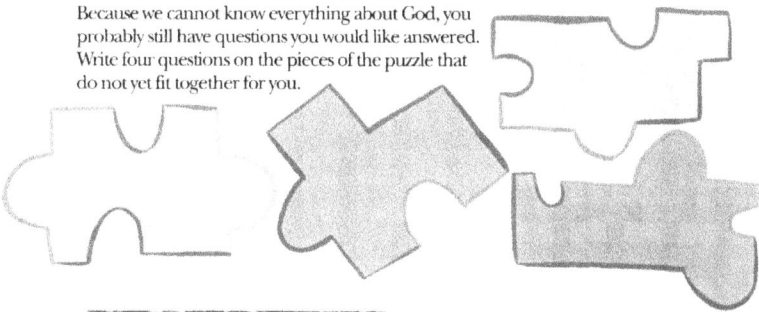

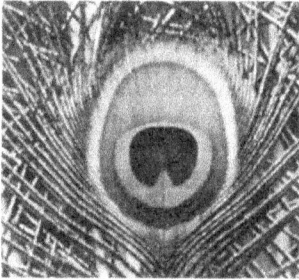

HINTS OF GOD'S TRUE WONDER

This is a very small part of one of God's creations. When we look at it, we get a hint of how wonderful the whole creation is.

Just as seeing a small part of one of God's creations gives us a hint of its full beauty, so each of God's creations can give us a hint of God's true wonder.

127

www.ingramcontent.com/pod-product-compliance
Lightning Source LLC
Chambersburg PA
CBHW050856150426

R18142900001B/R181429PG42813CBX00003B/1